P9-BIB-983

Praise for Angela Alioto

"A package of passion."

—Herb Caen, *San Francisco Chronicle*

"Angela has an almost encyclopedic knowledge of the issues."

—Kandace Bender, *San Francisco Examiner*

"[Her] humor, passion and hyperbole . . . are vintage Alioto"

—Savannah Blackwell, *San Francisco Bay Guardian*

"This woman has passion . . . she's an angel."

—Danny Glover

Abandon all hope, you who enter.

INFERNO, CANTO III

Straight to the Heart

Political Cantos

Straight to the Heart
Political Cantos

by Angela Alioto

RUSSIAN HILL PRESS
SAN FRANCISCO

Russian Hill Press, San Francisco
Printed in the United States of America
00 99 98 97 5 4 3 2 1

Book and jacket design by Kirk Franklin
This book is set in Jenson

Library of Congress Cataloging-in-Publication Data
Alioto, Angela.
  Straight to the Heart: Political Cantos / by Angela Alioto
      -1st ed.
[97-065290]
CIP
ISBN 0-9653524-2-0

Lisa Dahl, Margaret McNeal, and Jan Streck have each lost a child to the city of San Francisco. Because our current system failed these three women, they are all on their own private trips through Hell. In the hope that they come through to the other side safely, this book is dedicated in love and admiration to them.

CONTENTS

FOREWORD

THE DAY I MET ANGELA ALIOTO was a foggy one, but warm for the season. It was in San Francisco—North Beach, of course; and her father, who wanted to be the governor of California, was making the political rounds. She was being dragged along with her baby daughter, and behind her smile I detected a singular lack of enthusiasm for spending the day as a photo opportunity. She was going to college at the time, and trying to manage a small family. Politics was keeping her from doing what she really needed and wanted to do. She wasn't fazed by meeting any number of luminaries—Steve McQueen, Jerry Brown, Clint Eastwood. Politics was a means, not an end, for her. Back then, the end was to help her father.

These days, it's to change the world.

This is not to say that Angela has delusions of grandeur. Her greatest satisfaction comes from letters she gets from people she's helped, even indirectly. She's drawn to the types of issues and problems other politicians probably view as lost causes. When Angela turns her attention to a cause, it's not lost any more. She has taken on some of the most difficult issues and focused the spotlight of public scrutiny on them. What Angela realizes, and what mobilizes her, is that she has too much at stake, beginning with her own kids, to let a decent future pass us by. Angela's politics are based on common sense and vital issues like children, family, and safe schools and streets.

What is admirable about Angela's vision is that it's one that looks to the future. If Angela talks about the past, it is to illustrate what we can learn for the future. From the young woman with a baby balanced on her hip, reluctantly politicking, Angela has emerged as a strong, compassionate leader. No one else could have written this book, as Angela has an obligation—an obligation to get her message out there, to take aim at the heart of what has to be accomplished.

FRANCIS FORD COPPOLA
San Francisco
February 1997

ACKNOWLEDGMENTS

MY WORK ON THE San Francisco Board of Supervisors has been the most rewarding period of my professional life. The people I have known are the reason I'm devoted to public service, and they must be mentioned here, in no particular order: Sergio Lazzara, Robert Swall, Bob Pritikin, Harry Britt, Larry Nelson, Michael Cardoza, Terry Anderlini, and Sylvia Segal, Francisco Hsieh, Teresa Ferrer Guingona, George Millburn, Bruce Brugmann, Peter Bagatellos, Gino Lazzara, Myrna Diaz, Jim Clarke, Rich Mallonee, Brownie Mary, Eileen Hansen, Manny Valdez, John Hanley, Caroline Goodman, Orelia Langston, Francis Scarpulla, Michael Alioto, Bob Johnson, Patricia Cady, David Ferguson, Michael Farrah Jr., Shih-Wei Lu, Jamie Sanbonmatsu, Harvey Rose, Jim Hutchinson, Karen Licavoli, Kirk Kleinschmidt, Alyonik Hrushow, Sherri Chiesa, Larry Mazzola, Jim Salinas, Bill Hester, Alfonso Acampora, Paul Smoot, my good friend Russ Alley, and especially Sal Rosselli, who held my hand across the Abyss.

Throughout my term, I have been blessed with a phenomenal legislative staff, including Joyce Newstat, Michael Terris, Kira Sturney Keane, and Lester Olmstead-Rose. My special gratitude goes to Reg Smith and Jerry Windley, who stood by me through some hard times.

This book has been an exhausting but marvellous undertaking. Without the help of literally dozens of people, it would have been far more exhausting and far less marvellous. Joel Ventresca made sure I had my facts straight about PG&E. Mitch Fine is a bottomless source of political trivia—and important stuff. Phil Frank and Tom Meyer make San Franciscans laugh and think at the same time, and are generous enough to allow their work to appear in these pages. At Russian Hill Press, Anne Sheldon, Michael Vidor, Kit Cooley, Stephen Jamison, Kirk Franklin, Ted Knapp and especially Jeff Love turned words into a book. Francis Ford Coppola was a godsend in his support.

Finally, I must thank my children, who have stood by me during my eight years in office, including the last one, when writing this book occupied me far more than I had expected. Their comments and insights were invaluable, as were my father's—you're an inspiration, Dad.

POLITICAL CANTOS

I stand by this, my Comedy.

INFERNO, CANTO XVI

I N AUGUST 1996, during the writing of this book, I found myself in Dante's house in Florence. It is a beautiful place, that old house. I had been there before, and each time I'd been moved at the thought of Dante in exile from his beloved city, worrying about the state of Florentine affairs even after he had been banished from the city under pain of death.

As an explanation of his writing the *Commedia*, Dante wrote, "*Nel mezzo del cammin di nostra vita mi trovai in un bosco oscuro*"—"In the middle of the path of my life, I find myself in a dark wood." Dante's "dark wood" and mine are different, but I too find myself in the middle of life, needing to stop and share my thoughts about the nature of politics. I don't want to write a typical political "exposé," in which revelations about who slept with whom and who indulges in exotic vices are the rationale behind the writing. I'm more interested in what public office is really about: machine politics, the power of lobbyists and political consultants, campaign contributions and corporate influences, backroom deals at the public's expense, the promise of future paybacks for endorsements, and, most significant, the preservation of the status quo. When I mention names and relate specific instances, I'm trying to serve a higher purpose—to illustrate what is wrong (and sometimes right) with the way things work politically. And when I discuss local politics, I hope it's clear how this discussion reflects the national framework of politics.

This book is not an autobiography; it is a collection of cantos, or verses, of the hellish poem that is politics. I intend to go straight to the heart of the issue and share my thoughts about what I know, believe, and feel is wrong with the American political system. And though many of these stories are based on my experience in San

Francisco, they're relevant anywhere, to any American city or town. In this city, we have not been immune to the influences of power politics and a certain moral corruption, where the needs of special interests are met—often blatantly—at the public's expense. And if it happens in San Francisco, it happens everywhere.

I served on the board of supervisors of the city and county of San Francisco from 1989 to 1997. It's an influential post, as board legislation has often been replicated at the state and even federal levels, and for the past century many politicians have used this position as a springboard to state and federal office. In addition to being a San Francisco supervisor, I also served as board president for two years, from 1993 to 1995. I have served as the vice chair of the California Democratic Party and have been on the party's state executive board for 11 years. I also ran for mayor in 1991 and 1995.

It's a cliché to justify running for office by claiming a desire to do some good rather than a desire for power, but as I leave office because of term limits, I am comfortable with that explanation for my decision to serve the public. Machiavelli was right—not about the pursuit of personal power, but about the pursuit of power to bring about change. There is a difference.

I ran for mayor in 1991 because the mayor at that time, Art Agnos, was an arrogant man who often lacked the courage to do what was best for the city and its people. He refused to fund a crisis clinic that the city could not afford to lose, and he wouldn't support an emergency needle-exchange program to slow the spread of HIV in San Francisco. I ran for mayor again in 1995 because I was fed up with Mayor Frank Jordan's continued cuts to mental health and children's services and with his police-state tactics in dealing with the homeless. Both mayors could have done far better in handling the myriad of problems facing San Francisco, but they chose not to for a variety of reasons.

My primary interests have always been to protect the health and safety of the most vulnerable people among us—especially children, the poor, those with AIDS, and the mentally ill. I've fought tobacco interests because of the obvious harm they are doing to our country. I've fought to protect the heritage and environment of San Francisco (and therefore of California and America), to help small businesses survive, and to find ways to increase revenues for the city without increasing taxes.

Unfortunately, the problems of San Francisco and of the rest of the country have not gone away. A lot of them have gotten worse. Many of my colleagues and I have worked towards solutions, but most public officials have shown little interest in doing so. Too often, the best solutions offend those economic interests that have helped put the officials in office in the first place.

Over the years I've fought to stop the corruption in the awarding of municipal contracts; to open up the competitive bidding process; to go after the huge fees owed the city for more than half a century by Pacific Gas and Electric; to force the city to comply with federal laws that require it to supply its own electrical power to its own residents; to make the tobacco industry pay the medical costs of all tobacco-related illnesses; and to cut our bloated bureaucracy by a third. But these actions, of course, all anger powerful interests.

I didn't know they would when I started out, though I should have. After all, my dad is Joe Alioto, former mayor of San Francisco and one of the country's top political experts. I grew up with five brothers in an environment of prestige and influence. Our family name is synonymous with the history of the city, North Beach, and Fisherman's Wharf.

These are all realities, and I couldn't hide from them for political reasons, even if I wanted to. But I've never tried; I've never pretended to be anything I'm not. I was also raised not to see myself as different from anyone else. Because of the values instilled in me by my mother and father, I feel more comfortable with working mothers, the poor, the homeless, and other "typical" citizens than I do in the backrooms of politics where decisions are made in the interests of money and power. My study of St. Francis of Assisi—for whom San Francisco is named—helped mold my thinking a great deal. In confronting a political or social dilemma, I always try to ask myself what St. Francis would do in that situation.

I also feel a connection with immigrants and can understand their desire for a new start in America, which is why I've been so offended by the mean-spirited efforts of Governor Pete Wilson and his Proposition 187 supporters in California to punish those without voices or votes. My dad's father, Papa Alioto, was an immigrant. His parents put him on a ship to America when he was nine years old. After working in Milwaukee for two years at the railroad stations lighting gas lamps, he came to San Francisco and began working at Fisherman's Wharf. At 17, he went back to Sant' Elia, Sicily, to bring his parents, eight brothers, and one sister to America. He did this with the money he'd saved since he was nine.

My connection to San Francisco's history and cultural heritage must literally be in my blood: my grandfather met my grandmother on a fishing boat in San Francisco Bay during the 1906 earthquake. My grandmother's parents came from Termini Imerese, also in Sicily. She was born in San Francisco in 1893.

My mother's parents were also immigrants. My mother's father, Lorenzo Genaro, was born in Corleone, Sicily. As a youth he moved to Dallas, where he met my grandmother—whose family also came from Corleone.

My father and his three sisters were all born at 572 Filbert Street, near Saints Peter and Paul Church in the North Beach neighborhood of San Francisco. It was a big deal when Dad, the son of a Sicilian immigrant, became mayor. He wanted to pay tribute to his heritage, so he took all of us to Sicily to present the town of Sant' Elia with an organ he had bought for their little church. It was a gorgeous instrument, a real pipe organ, for this little town about the size of the Marina Green in San Francisco—the size of a couple of football fields. When we went to dedicate the organ, the whole town came out to greet him. There were banners, Madonnas, and a parade, all because Dad had become an important American.

There was a girl sitting in front of the *pasticceria*, the pastry shop. She was about my age, and she was knitting a sweater "*per gli americani*"—for the Americans. She was obviously poor. She wore tattered clothes and was caked with dirt; her feet were callused and bare. We grew up a world apart, but she had my face. At that moment I felt a newfound appreciation for Papa Alioto's leaving Sicily and coming to San Francisco. That could have been me sitting on that step selling sweaters to the Americans. I realized how lucky I was to be an American.

Some people might assume that because my father was mayor, I must have had politics in my blood, that I was raised to take back the reins of power in the family's name. Nothing could be further from the truth—though when I was little I thought I wanted to be a judge when I grew up. My father was an antitrust attorney. Though he was powerful locally and involved in politics, I wasn't really aware of it; to me he was just Dad. When he ran for mayor, I was already at the end of my senior year in high school. I was his biggest fan, and I went with him everywhere; I even wore Joe Alioto hats and passed out literature. I did it, however, because he was Dad—not because I was interested in politics.

When I did enter politics, though, it was because Dad had taught me that real change is possible, that democracy can work, and that it's up to each one of us to fight for what we believe.

I didn't learn politics directly from my dad. While I was growing up he tried to shield me from it, even though he was so visible in the media. Within a year he went from being an attorney to being San Francisco mayor to delivering Hubert Humphrey's presidential nomination speech at the 1968 Democratic National Convention. I was proud of him, but I remained uninterested in politics.

I married my late husband, Adolfo, when I was 18. I had first seen him three years earlier, at Good Friday mass. He'd just arrived from Italy and was wearing an Italian suit. I turned to my best friend, Valerie Atikian, and said, "See that guy over there? I'm going to marry him." Three years later, I did.

Adolfo and I had a storybook wedding. Afterwards I didn't stay home; I continued my college education. By the time I graduated I'd had two babies. I would take my oldest, Angela Mia, to my classes.

By the time I was 25, I had four children: Angela Mia, Adolfo, Joe and Gian-Paolo. Nothing's ever been more important to me than my children. I wanted to stay at home with them while they were little, but I also wanted to pursue a career in law. So I stayed at home until my youngest, Gian-Paolo, had started kindergarten.

I graduated from the University of San Francisco School of Law in 1983. After my graduation, my father wrote me a poem that says a lot about our relationship. Here are some lines from that poem:

> For Angela, a thunderous ovation,
> You made it to your law school graduation.
> The long-shot odds you started with were tough,
> But you had grit and stamina enough.
> Your sheepskin means the end of dreary school,
> No need now to bother with Shelley's rule.
> On to the courts to bust a trust or two.
> It's very good for commerce and for you.
> As student life draws to its happy end,
> This simple, soul-felt message I would send:
> I've loved you daughter mine, right from the start,
> Today my love just overflows my heart.

My parents both instilled in me an appreciation for the arts. My mother is a visual artist and Dad writes. Besides the graduation poem, he's written others and given readings in North Beach cafés. Dad read us the classics, including Dante and many others, when I was a child. He also reads the North Beach beat poets, who are part of San Francisco's heritage and were part of my own upbringing.

When I was 15, my parents took me to the Poets Festival in Spoleto, Italy. Dad was the festival director. I remember seeing Ezra Pound. Allen Ginsberg was there, too—getting arrested for reading a poem filled with profanity. The police had all been there waiting for him to break the law, which he did. It was my dad, in fact, who served as his attorney and got him out of jail—a lesson for me about the importance of fighting for individual rights.

On our trips to Italy, Dad would tell me stories about Dante walking down the streets of Ravenna, his home in exile, and how the little children would come running up to touch the cloak of *il poeta*. Elizabeth Barrett Browning's lines, "open my heart and you will see/ inscribed upon it *Italy*," made Florence come alive for me. She had lived around the corner from the school in Florence that I attended each summer. In summertime, my dad would bring a rose to her grave in the English cemetery. Dad loved the Romantic poets— Keats, Shelley, Byron, Browning—and passed that love on to me.

I grew up in an economically privileged family, but I still know what everyone goes through. I understand the difficulty women face trying to balance home and motherhood with work. I also understand what it's like to be a single mother. Through the years I've learned firsthand the importance of family, compassion for those who are sick, and the real issues involved with child care, health, and family leave policies.

When he was growing up, my son Adolfo was dyslexic. When I found out, I panicked and took him to the medical center at the University of California. The experts there didn't know what to do with him. Then one day a pediatrician told me to make him jump rope every day. He explained that jumping rope would help Adolfo use both sides of his brain. It did help. Two years ago Adolfo graduated from the Culinary Institute of Hyde Park (New York) with high marks. He's now an executive chef who's been lauded by restaurant critics. He's a genius in his own way.

My son Gian-Paolo had his share of obstacles growing up as well. When he was nine years old, my dad noticed that Gian-Paolo limped. Two of my brothers had had Legg-Calvé-Perthes disease as children, and Dad was worried. I took Gian-Paolo to La Scarpetta Hospital in Rome—we were on vacation at the time—and test results showed he had the disease. That was the beginning of a long three years, during which he had to wear braces on both of his legs. His braces made him strut like a cowboy, and the women in Italy would sometimes walk up and pat his head. Beyond his occasional complaint that "I can't stand these Italian ladies patting my head!" Gian-Paolo didn't let it stop him. When I was despairing because of his illness he'd say to me, "Come on, Mama. We're going to climb this mountain together, little buckaroo." All the doctors told us that Gian-Paolo would never be taller than five foot three. Today, my little buckaroo is just shy of six feet tall, and is a 20-year-old international business major at the University of Miami.

These experiences of motherhood helped me decide to make my way into public office. Part of what drives me is a kind of maternal concern for what I see around me—for the city, for the residents, for those most vulnerable.

My first stop on this road was a mid-1980s stint on the Catholic Commission on Aging. While on the Commission I worked to improve health care and safety for the elderly, among other things. This position gave me the opportunity to see the problems of the elderly firsthand and to look at some of the issues involved in the delivery of vital health services. During this time I also worked on an AIDS prevention video for teenagers in San Francisco, which put me into contact with HIV-positive children and convinced me that much more needed to be done to protect children and to improve AIDS services in the city.

In 1986 I accepted the co-chairmanship of the California Democratic Party platform committee. Two years later, I ran for supervisor for the second time (having run and lost in 1986), and was elected on November 8, 1988. The president of the board, Harry Britt, named me health committee chair, a position I went on to hold for six of my eight years on the board of supervisors.

In 1992, I was reelected to the board by such a wide margin that I was made president, a position in which I could make a difference. I quickly realized that I could introduce legislation on every issue I cared about. I could fight the tobacco lobby and win. I could fight for AIDS funding and win. I could fight for the youth and elderly and win. And I could fight for people with mental illness, disabilities, and substance abuse problems and win. In the two years I was board president, I introduced and passed more legislation than any other board president had in the history of San Francisco.

I fought against cutbacks in vital services, the closure of San Francisco General Hospital and the city's eight health care centers, the cuts in substance abuse programs, and for emergency needle exchange legislation. In trying to find economic solutions for these problems I grew intolerant of politics as usual—the payoffs and kickbacks that keep most politicians in office, that ensure the continued wealth of corporate and development interests, and that ignore the needs of the city's residents and its heritage.

For all these reasons and more, I ran for mayor twice—in 1991 and 1995. I'll never forget the day I announced my candidacy in 1995. We started out in North Beach outside Saints Peter and Paul Church, near the building where my father was born. There were over 500 people in attendance. My entire family was with me. Dad spoke, as did actor Danny Glover and writer and activist Ron Kovic, author of *Born on the Fourth of July*. All my oldest supporters were with me. We took cable cars from North Beach to Alioto Park in the Mission, then went to Bayview–Hunters Point, the Irish Cultural Center in the Sunset, and then back to the Marina. At each location we stopped and I announced my campaign. We ended up at Don Ramon's Restaurant, where the owner had a fabulous party.

The campaign was exciting and upbeat. I was doing well in the polls, coming in with over 25% in a large early field of candidates. But two months later, Willie Brown, assembly Speaker for 15 years and assemblyman for 30, announced that he was also running. Brown, who had the backing of the political establishment and millions of dollars, would prove impossible to beat. The political establishment would make sure he became the next mayor of San Francisco.

The campaign became negative; clearly, the political establishment didn't want to see me become mayor, because I rarely play ball with the establishment. I've always been outspoken. I say what I think because I believe it's necessary to tell people what's really happening politically. But running for mayor against Brown, I found myself powerless to stop the assault. I was fighting a powerful political machine that wanted Brown in San Francisco. I was fighting the pro-development interests that wanted to carve up the Presidio. I was fighting huge corporations that I had brought under intense scrutiny and were now backing Brown. Finally, I was fighting the tobacco industry, the same industry that had paid Brown more money in various contributions than any other politician in American history.

In his run for office, Brown raised some $3 million, an unheard-of sum for a mayor's race, even in a large city—which San Francisco is not. My campaign funds diminished as my financial base was devastated. With his money, Brown's campaign hired top people from the various political clubs around the city to help ensure that his name would appear on their slates. Later, after the election, many of these same people found themselves appointed to various positions in his administration.

Many of my supporters defected to Brown's camp. This was tough to bear, but I knew going into the race that politics was a dirty game. It also must have been difficult for my staff, who stood by me until I finally withdrew from the race. It was heartbreaking, but by mid-October 1995, I was down in the polls and had no money left. It was senseless to continue. I made the announcement that I was withdrawing and endorsed Roberta Achtenberg, a Clinton administration appointee who would have made city government more honest and efficient.

Achtenberg lost the primary to a well-financed Brown. With Brown as the sole opponent of conservative incumbent Frank Jordan, I had no choice but to endorse Brown. The endorsement was a matter of political necessity—anybody but a conservative. I couldn't bear the thought of four more years under Jordan, with his cruel anti-homeless policies. And my supporters felt the need to unite behind a liberal candidate.

Since taking office, Brown has brought verve and glamor to the city. Nonetheless, my worst fears have also been realized—the new mayor is an autocrat with more connections than a spider web. His brand of leadership discourages debate among other city leaders. He is arrogant and has already had to do something he rarely did in the state capital: apologize for offhand comments he's made. Important legislation that would have ensured fair bidding practices and necessary restraints on business and development have died under his watch. Campaign promises regarding the homelessness problem and public transportation have been broken due to Brown's inaction.

Being in public office builds a wall between most officials and the people they serve. It precludes compassion and an empathetic understanding of what people feel and experience. There is a temptation to rise above the "little people"—to become, with the newfound power of office, arrogant and aloof.

I've seen such arrogance, thoughtlessness, and lack of compassion time and time again, from the mayor's office on down the line. I've seen it shown toward mothers whose children have been murdered and who can't get the city to investigate. I've seen it in the callous, political decisions to defund crucial mental health programs. It's why I got involved in politics and why I'll continue to fight for what I believe, even though it's often a struggle.

My children understand this and have been wonderfully tolerant of my choices, but they can't believe what I go through. They've given up a lot of material comfort for me to be in politics, just as I have given up the opportunity to make a decent amount of money. Worse, for eight years I missed the opportunity to sit in court next to my father, one of the world's great trial attorneys. But all those regrets fade when I'm walking down the street and someone yells, "Give 'em hell, Angela."

But my children still recognize the insanity of public office. In 1992, in an attempt to keep the Giants from leaving the city, I sent a plan for a new ballpark to the team owners. My attempt to keep the team in San Francisco was widely reported in the newspapers. One day, in the midst of the press coverage, an old man walked up to me and shouted, "You're Angela Alioto! You're the jerk who wants to build the ballpark!" He hit me with his cane and walked away. Two of my children were with me when this happened; they just shook their heads and chalked it up to life with a politician.

More recently, I was with my daughter Angela Mia and some of my firefighter supporters in Marin County. I introduced myself to a woman and asked her to vote for me in the upcoming election. Angela Mia rolled her eyes. She's always thought that I am far too friendly with strangers.

The woman replied, "You're not Angela Alioto. I know Angela Alioto. You don't look a thing like her." Now it was my turn to roll my eyes.

This had happened before. I've had a weight problem since I stopped smoking in 1988, and politicians are constantly eating— there were some evenings during the mayor's race when I had *three* fundraising dinners to attend. People who saw me campaign in 1991 and in 1995 sometimes didn't recognize me in the later race. So when the woman added, "You're much fatter than Angela Alioto," the firefighters started snorting with laughter.

Finally I said, "You're right, I'm not Angela Alioto. But would you please do me a favor and vote for her?"

Angela Mia's eyes were rolling furiously by now.

My son Joe may have picked up his own peculiar facial habits from Angela Mia. In 1996, he attended the San Francisco Police Academy and served as president of his class. But he came to the house one day and told me he'd been reprimanded for exhibiting something called "facial expression attitude." As a public official, I suppose I should have taken the matter seriously, but in the circus of my life, it came across more as comic relief. I suggested to an administrator at the academy that if the only attitude they had gotten from Joe was from his facial expressions, then he must not have opened his mouth yet.

Where might my children have gotten their exasperation?

Politics has its good side—if it didn't, I wouldn't have stayed with it. It can be an opportunity to enact change that actually helps improve people's lives. I have always loved being an elected official. I love attending community meetings and discussing what we can do to make the city better. With the wonderful heritage and people of San Francisco, it's always possible to find a bit of joy. In addition to the parades and community celebrations, we sometimes get an opportunity to honor our heritage and have fun at the same time. We did this a couple of years ago in North Beach, when we celebrated the naming of a street after publisher and poet Lawrence Ferlinghetti.

The age of the beat poets is long gone. By the 1990s, bureaucrats were regulating coffeehouses and requiring special permits for poetry readings. Coffee shops and cafés that hosted recitals without a permit were being fined. But poetry and art are the lifeblood of cul-

15

ture and—especially when they are critical of social policies—an important reminder of our potential and our conscience.

So it seemed to me that the right thing would be for the city to honor its own poetic heritage. I asked the board of supervisors to rename a North Beach street after Ferlinghetti. The ridiculous nature of politics, however, meant that I had to spend 15 months trying to enact that simple name change. In the end, I had to locate a suitable street on my own. I finally found one that bureaucrats couldn't reasonably object to: Price Row, a tiny dead-end street that stretched maybe half a block. Ferlinghetti commented that the alley was "a fitting place for poets to hang out" since it had been used during Prohibition as a "back door for bootleggers."

Once I got approval, my dad planned a great celebration. We closed Columbus Avenue for the day and celebrated an Italian mass at Saints Peter and Paul Church. Several poets showed up and read their poetry. Allen Ginsberg sent a poem to be read. My dad wrote a poem commemorating Ferlinghetti's successful legal battle to publish Ginsberg's poem "Howl," which had been banned as obscene.

At the celebration, Ferlinghetti said, "The map of North Beach is stamped upon my brain pan. I know the streets and alleys like the palm of my hand. . . .It's truly unbelievable to have a tiny line in that palm named after me."

This is the way I, too, feel about San Francisco. I know the city like the palm of my hand. I know the problems that face its residents. I also understand how these problems translate into issues that every man, woman and child in America must grapple with.

My goal in writing this book was to discuss real issues and to let the public in on the surreal world of American politics. Voters may have some vague inkling of the notion of political corruption, but the ugly reality of politics is far worse than most people realize. It's closed doors, petty acts of political revenge, payoffs and campaign contributions. It's buying elections by trading promises for endorsements or paying back consultants by awarding huge contracts to the corporations for which they also lobby. I wanted to show a little bit of what it looks like from my perspective, to expose some of what's wrong with the system, and to describe some of the ways I believe it can be righted through public involvement.

When I was studying Italian and English literature at Lone Mountain College for Women (now the University of San Francisco), one of the texts that made a lasting impression on me was Dante's *Inferno*. After my years in politics I'm even more struck by the parallels between Dante's Hell and America's political quagmire. We do live in the midst of Hell without really recognizing it. As Dante did over 700 years ago, I have found that politics, like Hell, lies far beneath the surface of what is evident.

In writing this book, I wanted to show people just how far down that *beneath* goes. Dante's Hell has nine circles, some with several sections. Mine doesn't have as many, because our time is different and Dante would have punished people whom we now rightly praise—the gays and lesbians who speak out for equality, for example, or strong women. But between our time and Dante's there is a lot of common ground, and if Dante had been writing today, I believe he would find plenty of people and institutions to populate his map of Hell.

I wanted *everyone* to see what's going on at city hall, at the statehouse, and on Capitol Hill. The average person today has little idea to what depths those who govern often sink. She may grumble about her taxes, but she pays them. If the pothole in front of the house is filled and a policeman drives by occasionally, then perhaps everything is fine. But when do things cease to be fine? When the pothole remains? When the policeman appears less frequently? Or is it even later, when the house disappears down a sinkhole, or a child is shot while playing in the yard? Our political system is breaking down around us. In our poorest communities, there is no official system at all; who among us would willingly venture into South Central Los Angeles, or the South Bronx, or the poorest regions of the Mississippi Delta? The vast gulf between the haves and have-nots in America is the widest in the industrialized world, and it is growing every day.

My goal is to change the system. If, in reading this book, people open their eyes a little wider in disbelief at the proclamations of their elected officials, if they recognize the difference between an unpleasant political reality and the baloney that many elected officials prefer to dish out, then I will have accomplished my goal. If people recognize that the solutions to our current problems in government—and the problems we in government are trying to address—must extend beyond sound bites and ultrasimplified solutions and the scapegoating of the politically powerless, then I will have done in this work what I have set out to do my entire political life. At the same time, we all must remember that we *are* the government of this country, and its problems—and its occasional triumphs—are ours. Once we can all recognize that, it is my hope that the image of the political system as a Dantean Hell will begin to grow obsolete.

Until that time, however, I share this vision of Hell with you; like Virgil leading Dante through the Inferno, I'll hold you steady and keep you from stumbling, but I can't shield you from what lies ahead. And like Virgil and Dante, we will pass through it all to the other side, to see the stars.

THE UNCOMMITTED: PUBLIC "SERVANTS"

These of death
No hope may entertain; and their blind life
So meanly passes, that all other lots
They envy. . . .

INFERNO, CANTO III

THEODORE ROOSEVELT KNEW HIS DANTE. In the twilight of his career, searching for words to sum up his philosophy of life, he had to look no further than Dante's outer circle of Hell. In this special area, between the outer world and the hard-core damned in the deeper regions of Hell, are those nameless spirits who never made a choice. They spent their lives hedging their bets, swaying to and fro with each little breeze.

Roosevelt said:

> Far better is it to dare mighty things, to win glorious triumphs, even though checkered by failure, than to take rank with those poor spirits who neither enjoy much nor suffer much, because they live in the gray twilight that knows not victory nor defeat.

In a time when our leaders and statesmen and politicians ought to be showing great moral courage, most of them are instead taking stands like the one taken by Pilate, who also resides forever in Dante's outer circle. They wash their hands of the matter, choosing first one side and then the other, or neither, and in the interest of self-serving advancement, attempting only to placate the greatest number of people.

Government offices at all levels are filled by the ranks of Dante's uncommitted: the oblivious representatives who govern with no understanding of the needs of their constituents; the rubber-stamp politicians who fear that any independent act on their part will result in their being abandoned by moneyed interests; the waffling officials whose pants seats are filled with slivers from sitting on the fence; the detached bureaucrats who rigidly follow the narrow rules created by those in political power; the civil servants who respond to human crises only until the end of the workday; and the civic leaders, blind to human need, who fail to understand the impact of their often stupid and selfish actions on the lives of others.

These "poor spirits" represent everything that's wrong with American politics. I don't know which category's worse. The examples range from the ridiculous to the tragic. We can see their handiwork in political opposition to projects as simple as trying to form a youth commission, or get a film commission established to promote business interests, or attempting to rename a street after Lawrence Ferlinghetti to honor San Francisco's poetic heritage. And we can also see it in something as grim as fighting police opposition to tracking down a killer.

Such things happen every day in every city across this country. They happen in state legislatures when our elected officials pass mean-spirited laws and budgets that punish those who have no power to speak out. They happen in Congress, especially in election years, when senators and representatives consistently vote in favor of guns and pork barrels over butter. And they happen in the Oval Office when presidents abandon those who elected them in favor of pandering to the most recent polls.

Hand-washing has become synonymous with politics.

Former San Francisco Mayor Art Agnos might be found outside the gate.

In July 1991, the $2.9 billion city budget was being finalized, short $240,000—the amount needed to keep Mt. Zion Crisis Clinic open.

San Francisco could never have afforded to operate Mt. Zion without help. Top doctors and interns from the University of California and from San Francisco General Hospital volunteered around the clock, providing free care to 6,000 patients a year. Most of the patients were minorities, homeless, people with AIDS, or 5150s—people with psychiatric disorders who pose a risk to themselves or others. Few of them could ever have paid for the kind of treatment they got. And Mt. Zion was our only 24-hour crisis clinic, the kind of place people can go in the middle of the night if they're scared of dying. If you walked through the doors of Mt. Zion, you'd see the mentally ill as well as young people who had overdosed on drugs. And they would all get taken care of.

At that time I was serving as chair of the board of supervisors' health committee (a position I held for six of my eight years in office), and the Mt. Zion closure was a critical issue to me. This wasn't the only public health issue that Agnos and I fought over, but it was the most crucial.

I was committed to keeping Mt. Zion open, but Agnos was ready to block funding and force it to close. His excuse was that the methods employed by doctors at Mt. Zion were ineffective, but in truth he was going to allow funding to disappear because his ego would not allow him to let Mt. Zion stay open. He had responded to my fight to keep the facility open by publicly demanding its closure, and he was too arrogant to back down.

The city could not afford to lose Mt. Zion over such petty politics. Desperately sick people would have nowhere to go.

So, as health committee chair, I called a hearing on the closure, and 500 people showed up. Every major ethnic and social group was represented, as was every neighborhood. A couple from Pacific Heights testified that their son had freaked out one night after taking some Ecstasy and had been taken to Mt. Zion for treatment. A single working mother from Bayview had taken her daughter there after she had been raped. A formerly homeless man from the Mission district testified that Mt. Zion had saved his life.

Two-thirds of those who were served by Mt. Zion were minorities. Nevertheless, there were minority supervisors on the board who voted to close it, because Agnos had called them and told them to do so.

I argued that many of those being served were homeless, and, with no place to go if they got into trouble, they'd be picked up as 5150s. The cops, with no Mt. Zion to take them to, would simply drop them in alleys, where they'd become either murder victims or criminals themselves.

There's a thin line between sanity and insanity. Unfortunately, politicians don't see this fact. Mental health services get cut every year because politicians don't acknowledge that mental illness exists. Apparently it plays better in the press to label it a character flaw or a lifestyle choice. Although the supervisors would never cut cardiac care at San Francisco General Hospital, they are willing to reduce the numbers of beds for psychiatric care every year. And so every year there's a fight to restore those beds. In San Francisco we usually keep a minimum of $10 million in the budget's reserve fund, and for years I was forced to allocate about a million of it for mental health programs that had been cut.

Places like Mt. Zion Crisis Clinic are the only places that can make a difference in the lives of our most at-risk citizens. If they close, almost all of these people will end up in jail, on the streets— or dead. Yet, given the consequences of service cuts, funding for mental health has always been an uphill battle. Now here was the mayor closing down an important symbol of prevention.

I told Agnos if he closed Mt. Zion, I'd run against him for mayor. He didn't believe me. Nor did he restore funding for the clinic. So, on August 8, 1991, I announced my candidacy.

It was far too late in the game, though. Looking back, I can see that I should have taken the money I spent on the race and simply given it to Mt. Zion to stay open—the amount would have just about covered it.

Two weeks after the general election, I was in a car accident. I'd hit my face on the steering wheel, cut my lip, and was taken to San Francisco General Hospital. While I was in the recovery room with my dad and my children, both Frank Jordan and Art Agnos visited me. When I woke up from surgery and saw those two, I thought I'd died and gone to Hell. Each brought me flowers, and each wanted

COURTESY OF TOM MEYER

my endorsement in the runoff election. They each believed that my endorsement would decide the outcome of the race.

In 1991, I had adopted another crucial issue—needle exchange. By that point it was obvious that needle-exchange programs reduced the spread of HIV among drug users and their sexual partners. If users had access to clean needles, they wouldn't be forced to share, and the spread of HIV could be reduced. Stopping the spread of HIV was critical in San Francisco; we'd been hit harder than any other city in America, and drug users were at terrible risk. But these proposals were considered radical at the time, and right-wing politicians throughout California claimed that needle-exchange programs would only promote drug use. Public health experts, though, saw needle exchange as a method of "risk reduction" that could slow the spread of HIV and save lives.

But few politicians listen to health experts—it makes better press to champion the war on drugs than to take care of "junkies."

To provide clean needles to drug users, we had to legalize the practice, and to do that, San Francisco had to declare a state of emergency with the city's health department. Agnos had refused, thinking he would lose popular support. He decided to not do the right thing rather than face the political fallout. For him, as for many other politicians, it was easier to sway in the breeze than to fight it.

Now that he and Jordan were facing a runoff election, Agnos was asking for my endorsement. He and I had split the progressive vote in the city. Jordan had come in first with 62,084 votes, Agnos had come in second with 53,085, and I had come in third with 35,917. If he could get my support, he figured he would be a shoo-in for reelection.

But I felt that Agnos had betrayed me and the people that had elected him. There was the needle-exchange debacle, for one thing. But Agnos had also showed his arrogance in opposing me—and ignoring the good of the city—on the creation of the film commission, which August Coppola had first proposed to me. Though my ordinance creating the commission finally passed, and Coppola ran the commission for two years, he eventually quit because of Agnos's continual underfunding of the program. Agnos, unwilling to follow someone else's lead in a political matter, had tried to defeat a program that has since pumped millions of dollars into San Francisco's economy.

Still, as arrogant as he was, I felt Agnos was much better for the city than the more conservative Jordan. So despite my anger and feelings of betrayal, I told Agnos I was willing to support him if he would return to his progressive roots and declare the state of emergency needed for the needle-exchange program.

He refused again.

Two days later I was visited by Jordan and his political consultant, Jack Davis. They knew of my political battles with Agnos and wanted my endorsement as well. I withheld my endorsement of Agnos, and Jordan promised the city he would declare the state of emergency if he was elected mayor.

Art Agnos was not reelected.

Somehow, Jack Davis got Frank Jordan, a conservative former cop, elected mayor of the most liberal big city in America. A month after taking office, Jordan signed my needle-exchange legislation. It was one of the few progressive, courageous acts he was to carry out as mayor.

Unfortunately, there was no chance to get used to surprises like that. The new mayor's single-term tenure in San Francisco was riddled with incompetence.

My progressive allies and I found ourselves in a four-year fight with Jordan over funding programs crucial to the well-being of San Franciscans, especially those most in need. Jordan turned out to be a miniature Pete Wilson, tossing a crumb here and there to civic-minded people, but heartless in denying help to the poor and sick and refusing to buck the downtown business interests. Every year he slashed the budget for either clinics, outreach programs or children's centers, and every year the board slapped him in the face with overrides. He waffled so much he could have opened a pancake house.

One summer, Jordan defunded a community children's center in the Mission district, an area that is home to thousands of working-class poor and their children. A neighborhood community activist took me to investigate, and I came away with my head spinning. The center was responsible for the care of some 20 children, all of whom were younger than three years old. Some had HIV. It was a tragic situation, yet the four women taking care of the children were doing a fabulous job. And by having this center, the mothers—mostly teenagers—could go to school, get training, or find work.

I have four children of my own. I hug them, I adore them, and I raised them as well as I could. I think they turned out great, thanks to a lot of hard work and luck, and by the grace of God. But these children in the Mission wouldn't ever have much luck. And the hard work that was necessary to give them a chance to grow up at all was in danger of being defunded by a politician that didn't get it.

In my years as a supervisor I've tried to make sure that funds for this and other programs like it weren't cut, but despite my success in keeping the Mission children's center open, I've been fighting a political system that has become more about starting fires, ignoring people's needs, and making headlines than about helping people.

An unfortunate by-product of uncommitted politicians is the existence of uncommitted bureaucrats. Much like their elected counterparts, they rarely take action that requires creativity or risk. And because bureaucrats are appointed and often outlast their appointers, they grow even more comfortable sitting on fences.

While we must be cautious about jumping on an all-encompassing antibureaucracy bandwagon, we should be aware of the monolithic nature of bureaucracy as a whole. All government services are provided by bureaucracies, and without them, nothing would get done. But bureaucracy relies heavily on rules and procedures, and rules and procedures can prevent many bureaucrats from taking the risk of doing the right thing. Bureaucracy also exists largely to perpetuate itself rather than to serve the public. It should not be surprising to us that bureaucrats are people with a vested interest in keeping their jobs.

In every civic situation, we see bureaucrats enforcing permits beyond reason, creating red tape for those seeking disaster relief and slowing the pace of police investigations. A common perception, and unfortunately an accurate one, is that bureaucracies often fail to act with compassion in the face of tragedy, and that they ignore human needs when a few simple actions could save lives and ease suffering. Lack of flexibility means lack of heart, creativity, understanding and vision.

Nearly every year in San Francisco the number of psychiatric beds for mentally ill patients gets cut. In addition, the number of homes in the community for the mentally ill continues to decline. At one time there were more than 300 such homes. Now we're down to a fourth of that number. So it's obvious we've got a problem. And given the small number of facilities that still exist in the city to house the mentally ill, it would seem that we could do something to bend the rules instead of making them more rigid. But a lot of bureaucrats like them rigid. And rules and red tape are often used as an excuse to reduce the number of such facilities, which is unconscionable.

One program that should never have been cut was the Center for Special Problems, a residential and outpatient facility that served a number of violent, mentally ill ex-cons. The city health department decided that the state or federal government should pay for the facility, since its patients were criminals. If we had not fought hard to keep it running, the clinic would have closed immediately without even being granted the time to find replacement services for its clients, including some who were murderers. Violent people who needed counseling would have been put out on the street because of bureaucratic bickering.

Another distressing example is the fate of Chateau Agape, run by Cathy and Leroy Looper. These two modern-day St. Francises had turned their house into a home for the mentally ill. While they were struggling to keep Chateau Agape open, the city planning department was busy making life impossible for them, requiring that their facility, an old Victorian mansion, be fitted with a new roof—to the tune of $90,000.

Rules are obviously made for a reason, and the original reasons behind most of them are sound. But in this case the rule was an unnecessary obstacle. Chateau Agape was going to have to close its doors because it couldn't pay for renovations on a roof that didn't even need safety work. If it comes down to enforcing the rule, even at the expense of losing a critical facility, well. . .rules can also be bent, if you take all factors into account.

I went to work on Cathy's and Leroy's behalf, trying to loosen the permit regulations. I met with parents whose children were being served by Chateau Agape and heard from them about the horror of watching your child go through high school, getting good grades and just being a typical child, then waking up one morning and finding a stranger where your child had been. Mental illness is terrifying. The hell and the agony and the pain that parents endure is unimaginable. Those parents had the added burden of not knowing what would happen to their children if Chateau Agape closed down. The way they saw it, city government didn't recognize mental illness as a disease, and city bureaucracies didn't recognize any responsibility beyond a rigid application of the rules and regulations.

Chateau Agape is now closed.

This book is dedicated to three women who have lost children to violence. One of these mothers, Lisa Dahl, has become a good friend. Lisa's son was Justin Jones, a 23-year-old who lived in Marin County, a suburban community north of San Francisco. He was the same age as my son Joe. One day, Justin rode his bike down to the Haight-Ashbury district to go to a record store. While on Haight Street, he saw a man grab a knapsack from a blind man on the corner and then run away down the street. Justin, being the kind of person that he was, rode his bike after the man. But when he caught up with the man and grabbed the knapsack, the man turned and stabbed Justin in the heart, killing him. After his death, Justin came to be known as the "Good Samaritan."

Lisa Dahl came to see me two days later and brought with her Jeannie Boyle and Mackenzie Green, a private investigator. Jeannie is a well-known criminal artist; she had done the drawing of Richard Allen Davis, Polly Klaas's killer. The private eye began investigating the crime, because Chief of Police Anthony Ribera said he didn't have enough people to do it. They weren't investigating witnesses; they weren't doing anything. There was no "overtime" money in the budget.

As the mother of four children, I knew that Lisa Dahl must have been living through an unimaginable nightmare. If one of my children were killed, I'd wonder if life were worth continuing. But Justin was Lisa's *only* child—how does she manage to go on?

If anything was going to give Lisa the strength to live, it was going to be finding her son's killer. Jeannie did a portrait of him, and I called for hearings.

At the hearings about the investigation of Justin's murder, the head of the homicide division, Earl Saunders, said, "We don't have enough money to work nights and weekends to interview witnesses." Now, I can't express my level of rage at a system that allows a mother to go through this, and then to hear that there is not enough money to find out who killed her son. Can you imagine sitting in a hearing, listening to a cop—a good cop—say, "We can't go and interview and find out who killed your son, because we don't have enough money in the budget," especially when so many cops are sitting at desks shuffling paperwork? And meanwhile, we have political leaders whose main concern is making corporate deals that take millions of dollars away from the city budget—money that could be spent on investigating the murder of people like Justin.

But the political fact is that there isn't the money in the budget, and police and others must find a way to do the job with the budget they have. That means getting people out from behind desks and onto the streets. Cutting bureaucracy will mean that resources can go farther. Just as a clinic health care provider should be providing care and not filling out forms, a police officer should be protecting citizens.

I knew that the odds for finding Justin's killer would be improved if we could offer a substantial reward for information leading to his arrest and conviction, so I approached Mayor Jordan about offering one. When he refused to allocate any money at all for a reward, I pressed the board of supervisors to set aside $10,000.

Finally, under the harsh spotlight of the hearings, the police department agreed to allocate resources to the investigation. They found Justin's murderer two months later. He was tried, convicted, and sentenced to 16 years to life. The informants who turned him in did so for the reward.

Lisa has since moved to Arizona, where she has opened a restaurant. On the menu is a photo of Justin and a dedication to him. Without the arrest of her son's killer, she might not have been able to do any of this. And in the Haight, where he was stabbed, a city mural dedicated to Justin will be completed in 1997.

Margaret McNeal is an African American woman who lives in the poor, working-class San Francisco neighborhood of Bayview–Hunters Point. Her daughter Alexius was shot in the head in her home, and her body was then stuffed into a closet. She was 13 years old. Margaret had heard of Lisa Dahl's case, and she called me to see what I could do in helping to find her daughter's killer. After I went to Alexius's funeral and met with Margaret, I contacted Frank Jordan and was able to get approval for a $10,000 reward.

The killer was found and convicted, despite the difficult logistics of solving any kind of crime in a poor African American neighborhood. Earl Saunders, who was recently appointed deputy chief of police, attributed the solution of the case to the reward money.

After this case I co-authored a city charter amendment that requires full staffing and funding for the police force. It is one of my most important pieces of legislation and has nipped in the bud any possible funding-related excuses for not throwing the full weight of the police behind an investigation.

A blindness to human need and suffering often afflicts both bureaucrats *and* politicians, as in the case of the murder of Tony Ray. Here the coroner takes a prize for thoughtlessness. Tony was the victim of a vicious Polk Gulch murder. However, unlike Justin, the "Good Samaritan," Tony had been a runaway from Iowa, a hustler trying to survive on the streets. After Tony's murder, his mother, Jan Streck, came to town to see what was being done to find her son's killer. The police were investigating, but the city wouldn't increase the reward of $10,000.

Jan came to my office. By this time, I'd established a reputation for getting resources allocated to investigations like this. I again went to Jordan for help, but he refused to increase the size of the reward. Tony was a hustler, a self-made victim. Jordan might have seen championing a male prostitute by issuing a decent reward as a political risk. What he didn't understand in washing his hands of the matter was that a woman's child is her child, no matter what he may have done. If the conditions of our society allow or force a person to turn to an unsavory lifestyle, are we then going to turn our backs on that person? Tony was murdered while he was doing what he needed to do to survive on our streets.

33

Jan went back home to Iowa to await the release of her son's body from the coroner's office. Because she could not afford to have the body transported for burial, the coroner finished the examination and had Tony cremated.

Now for the unthinkable part. Without informing Jan, the coroner told the funeral home to box up Tony's ashes and had them sent to her by Federal Express. The following day, Jan's doorbell rang and she opened the door, signed a form for a package from San Francisco, and was handed the box.

What would a person's reaction be upon opening a box like that?

If I were Jan, I'd have sued the city for every penny I could get out of them. As an elected official of the city, I'm still ashamed that this happened. No one involved in that decision deserves to have their job today. What kind of government would do that? Certainly not a civilized one. Of course, rules were invoked, and everyone tried to cover themselves. As Jan said later, none of it is going to bring her son back, but only by calling attention to such behavior do we have the hope of ending it.

The system doesn't work when the coroner of a city sends a mother the ashes of her son by Federal Express, without warning. It doesn't work when it underfunds and overbureaucratizes the police department. It doesn't work when it balks at providing rewards substantial enough to help solve crimes and prevent further murders. It doesn't work when a convicted, recidivistic, violent criminal like Richard Allen Davis is out on the streets in the first place, able to murder Polly Klaas.

The system doesn't work when it sentences Tony Ray to death in the streets.

Pain and suffering aren't going to go away. The most streamlined and compassionate government in the world couldn't bring that about. But the fundamental question we must ask ourselves is, what is government *for*, exactly?

What government ought to do is take care of its citizens. If you eliminate every other consideration—the pettiness, the self-serving and self-perpetuating politics, the lust for power—and focus on service, you have a good start. If we can make bureaucrats and politicians remember that they're public *servants*, then we've taken a step in the right direction.

One of the most popular (and tired) excuses by public officials, whether elected or appointed, is that "rules are rules." One of the problems with rules, however, is that they are often enforced in ways that lack compassion and an understanding of exceptions. Human tragedy is an obvious case in point. California has more than its fair share of catastrophes—earthquakes, floods and drought, fires—and they affect an enormous number of people. And the rest of this continent-sized country of ours is continuously in one disaster season or another. When a disaster hits, whether in the flood plains of the Mississippi, the hurricane belt of the East Coast, or the Midwest's "Tornado Alley," we need leeway and flexibility in order to help the victims. And when a personal disaster strikes, there's similarly an opportunity for compassion, for speeding up the system or using the tools of government to help reduce suffering.

From my own experience, however, this does not always happen. Sometimes bureaucrats just remain bureaucrats, and public officials stubbornly refuse to make anything easier for people. Sometimes, rules aren't just rules.

They're obstacles.

Blindness to human needs can be seen in the response to personal disasters, in the things that seem unimportant to bureaucracies. In one case, the San Francisco coroner, toeing the "rules" line a little too closely, decided it would be unlawful to release the body of a Chinese girl, who had drowned at Ocean Beach, to her family for a

Buddhist ceremony. Instead, the coroner wanted the body held for an autopsy, which the family opposed on religious grounds.

I was contacted by the family and was shocked that the bureaucratic rules allowed no room in this case for compromise—for compassion in the face of human need. No attention was being paid to the family's grief. I called the coroner and asked him to allow the family to perform their religious ceremony. He refused, and the family was forced to go to court. The judge agreed with them, and the girl's body was released so the ceremony could be performed.

One of the pleasures of holding elected office is the ability to legislate changes that loosen regulations a bit and, by so doing, ease human suffering. In the days following the Loma Prieta earthquake, which caused serious damage throughout San Francisco and ravaged the posh Marina district, the city was full of people who wanted to rebuild. They didn't want to build something new or different—they wanted what they had had the day before the earthquake. That didn't sound out of line to me.

I hurried through some legislation for issuing rebuilding permits, an action for which I was roasted alive by some tenants' groups. Though I have been their staunchest ally in San Francisco, they were screaming that the legislation favored homeowners; since homes in San Francisco are so expensive, this legislation was seen as aid to the wealthy. But the legislation called for the allocation of emergency earthquake permits to anyone residing anywhere, including in illegal apartments, who wanted to rehabilitate their home and restore it to its prequake condition. The legislation also took into account the mental state of those who'd been devastated, showing that compassion can indeed become a part of the political system.

I also created legislation to loosen the general process of getting permits, which had become nearly impossible to obtain. If you want to put an extra bathroom in your house, you ought to be able to do so without a lot of hassle. But government agencies have become so rigid and compartmentalized and bound in red tape that the building permit process had become a frustrating obstacle. Anyone seeking a permit had to go from building to building and room to room in city government. A few even had to hire attorneys to help them. This maze of regulations also made the entire system vulnerable to bribery and extortion. There are lawyers in this town who've made a living from doing end runs around the permit system.

The permit system in San Francisco exemplified the way most city governments are run—as a morass of rules, tangling up, rather than assisting, anyone who tries to ask for help. Rules had replaced common sense, and the bureaucracy had grown into a monster incapable of examining either individual cases or itself. So I took a piece of legislation created by San Francisco Supervisor Nancy Walker and amended it so that we could set up a one-stop permit system. Sure, homeowners should have to go through official channels to ensure that something valuable is not being destroyed; but there should be only one such channel , and it ought to be a straightforward one to get through.

So far, this system—and many others around the country—hasn't been repaired.

How far will public "servants" go in the name of compassionless regulation, or in the interest of self-perpetuation? When does a bureaucratic or political decision cross the line from merely senseless to truly harmful to the community? One result of the Loma Prieta earthquake in San Francisco was serious structural damage to some famous old churches in the city. San Francisco Archbishop John Quinn used the damage as a poor excuse to permanently close many of these churches, claiming that the archdiocese lacked the funds to retrofit. Sensing he had the momentum, perhaps, Quinn also decided to close certain other churches, citing declining church attendance and contributions. In all, nine churches closed their doors.

A decision came down from Quinn's office that the properties would be sold.

Now, everyone knows that the value of San Francisco real estate is in orbit somewhere above the Earth. So Quinn was making an informed *economic* decision that churches were going to close, and worshippers were going to lose their churches and have to go farther away on Sundays. Some San Franciscans had attended the same church all their lives. They'd been baptized and married there. On top of that, many of the churches represent a piece of San Francisco history. Several of them are architecturally beautiful and add an incalculable value to the city's character. So closing them is more than a matter of inconveniencing a few people; Quinn was proposing to change something basic about San Francisco.

Among the churches slated for closure was St. Thomas More, which was packed at every Sunday Mass. All Hallows was one of the few Catholic churches in the poor Bayview–Hunters Point neighborhood. It's a tiny building; it wouldn't have cost much to fix it. It, too, was closed. St. Francis of Assisi in North Beach was California's first parish church. When it closed, its parishioners tried to get a priest to open it up on his own and take responsibility for it. St. Brigid's needed retrofitting to the tune of $6 million. The parishioners agreed to raise the money, but Quinn wanted that church sold. It has been closed for over a year at this writing.

I spent time in college studying church architecture both in San Francisco and Florence, Italy, so I know something about it. Every one of the churches marked for closure fell into at least one of two categories: it was architecturally and historically valuable, or it was still serving the spiritual needs of people in its community. For the representative of the Catholic Church in San Francisco to decide that the church coffers were more important than the needs of the community was compassionless beyond understanding. Church leaders should consider themselves "public servants" in every sense of the term, as Saint Francis did, yet the church is as political as any governing body, with its rules and regulations and self-perpetuating interests. It serves as an example, in this case, of what's wrong with our civic leaders.

I joined the outraged Catholic community in their objections to Archbishop Quinn's decisions. We held protests and demanded the reopening of all the churches. I also became an honorary member of the Catacomb Group, which rotates their meetings from church to church to keep from being discovered since the archbishop has forbidden them to meet on church property. All we wanted was to keep the churches open.

I finally planned to introduce legislation to earmark the churches for historic preservation. The churches clearly needed the protection, and it wasn't an outrageous idea—but it stepped on toes.

When the archbishop heard about the legislation, he flipped his lid over the potential loss of millions of quick and easy dollars, and he had the gall to call my *father* rather than deal with a "hysterical" woman.

My father called me, a little amused, knowing how I'd react. "Sure, Dad, you go see the archbishop," I told him.

> But if your son John was the parent of four terrific children, an antitrust attorney, president of San Francisco Board of Supervisors—the second most powerful position in the city—do you think the Archbishop of San Francisco would have called *his* daddy? I don't think so.

Quinn's going to my *daddy* to complain about me convinced me that San Francisco's archbishop was totally out of touch with anyone real. But I told my dad he could deal with Quinn if he wanted.

So Dad told Quinn that I was right in what I was doing, and that he ought to take it up with me personally if he had a problem.

At that point the archbishop realized he'd need the help of politicians and bureaucrats similarly committed to self-preservation and the monetary bottom line. So he called then-assembly Speaker Willie Brown and asked him to pass state legislation that took away the right of any city—including San Francisco—to declare landmarks on the local level. The support of the church is important to the powers-that-be in Sacramento; Brown wasn't about to alienate a Catholic archbishop.

The legislation, which passed the assembly, took away the ability of local government to make decisions for itself. So some faceless assemblyman from Orange County now has the power to determine whether St. Brigid's in San Francisco deserves to be made a historical landmark. It's not just a bad rule—it's insulting. It implies we can't make decisions for ourselves.

The new archbishop, William Levada, is more sensitive to the issue and has been more willing to talk with angry parishioners. Many of the churches, such as All Hallows and St. Thomas More, have been reopened. The church of St. Francis is to be made into a national shrine, and St. Joseph's will become a homeless shelter. But signs nailed to the doors of the rest of the churches tell passersby that sales are pending. Holy Cross, in the outer Fillmore district, and St. Benedict, in Laurel Heights, have been sold. The real estate is valuable, after all, and it wouldn't do to have churches that are closed anyway just taking up space.

They don't do any good, sitting there with closed doors. The poor can't even get inside on cold days to warm themselves up.

Nothing new, right? We all know that the government is just a big bureaucracy, that it makes money disappear and doesn't produce the things we, as citizens, have a right to expect.

That is, of course, an oversimplification. The sentiment reflects the general feelings of a disgruntled public. When we scream for less government, we don't really want less government at all. We want the services government provides. We want public television so that there's worthwhile children's programming, school lunches for poor children who might not otherwise have a meal during the day, a decent and safe ride on public transportation, and Medicaid so that the elderly and the poor can receive needed medical treatment.

What we really want is a more user-friendly government. A simpler interface. Less hassle. Fewer rules. The government should be taking care of us more than it takes care of itself. Its existence should be dedicated solely to helping people who need help—and that's everyone, at one time or another.

The anger people feel towards the government comes from somewhere. There is a deep-seated belief that government isn't working. And without calling for armed overthrow of our elected leaders, we can pinpoint what is good about government—what works—and we can apply solutions to the problems.

Rules must be treated as guidelines rather than as biblical commandments. Rules are in place to help people, to ensure rights, and to prevent abuses. When rules are invoked as a hindrance, we must speak out against it. When a rule doesn't work, it must be thrown out. *Change* shouldn't be a dirty word if what it refers to is something that will help people, that will prevent the excesses of a self-serving bureaucracy, and that will restore in *public servants* a sense of their original purpose.

THE LUSTFUL, THE GLUTTONOUS
AND THE AVARICIOUS:
THE POLITICAL MACHINE

A wretched, godless crew.

INFERNO, CANTO VI

THE FIRST CIRCLE OF HELL after the realm of the Uncommitted is Limbo, in which Dante placed the virtuous unbaptized. Homer and Ovid and other great men who didn't have the good fortune to die as Christians spend eternity here—not really being punished, but not being allowed into Heaven, either. Dante's not too critical of them, and, in truth, their exclusion from Heaven is typical of late medieval thinking, which is narrow and church-centered by our contemporary standards. But all in all, these souls made out okay, considering Dante.

Not so with the damned in the next four circles.

Those who committed the sins of appetite were doomed to spend eternity in punishments reflecting their sinful lives. They lusted, they ate and drank to excess, they were greedy for power and money—habits that even today we consider distasteful at best.

Politics today is dominated by people hungry for power and has been since the birth of the concept of *politics*. Dante would have said these people suffered from excessive cupidity. Though the desire to help others can't be discounted as the motive for many committed men and women in the political arena, it's an obvious fact that the spotlight draws people who *crave*. They are not active in the world of politics out of a sense of civic duty, or a desire to change the world for the better. They are in it for the power and the money and all the things associated with making headlines and policy.

When you have a political system made up of enough people of this kind, as we do in America, you have an entity that begins to take on a life of its own. Made up of politicians and the people and organizations who funnel money to campaigns, these huge creations become, both literally and figuratively, *machines*. Examples include

Huey Long's Louisiana machine of the 1930s or the New York bosses who ran their boroughs with an iron fist for much of the last two centuries. In California, politicians must sooner or later come to terms with what is called the "Burton machine," named after Congressman Phil Burton, who died in 1983.

When I first ran for political office in 1986, I had no idea of the extent of the political machine's power. I never would have imagined that a few elected officials in local and state government could effectively control politics at so many levels. I certainly wouldn't have expected that the Burton machine would still be alive and well years after the death of its namesake. Over the past ten years, not only have I learned that the Burton machine still exists, but I have experienced firsthand the kind of power the machine wields in politics at all levels.

If the Burton machine is any example, machines obtain and extend their power through a variety of means. They use a system of political patronage to create a family of loyal elected officials. Locally, those loyal to the machine are groomed for political office in exchange for the promise that, if elected, they'll follow the machine's lead in making key political decisions. This loyalty can result in guarantees of campaign money. Machines help establish finance committees and tap big contributors, who can be located with a few well-placed calls and who, more often than not, will implicitly trade money for the promise of votes on key issues. Machines can also provide important endorsements, which bring in money as well as volunteers. As endorsements build, other organizations, politicians, and unions get on board to avoid being punished later by being left out of the political process should the machine candidate win.

This process translates into paybacks, since the machine may "unofficially" request from the newly elected official the power to name the key appointments that are under the new politician's control. These might be top administrative appointments in the government or local or state committee slots in the political party. In this way, top appointments are often given to individuals who were influential in delivering contributions or organizational endorsements. In turn, machine appointments to local or state party committees help ensure the continued power of the machine.

This system of favors and paybacks comes with a price. Like borrowing from a loan shark, newly elected officials are never free from this debt. Their continued loyalty is expected, and this loyalty includes how they vote. They'll be expected to support certain legislation on behalf of the machine and oppose other legislation. Although some of this legislation is issue related and may in fact coincide with the official's own political persuasion, other expected votes might well be designed to protect powerful machine contributors. At a minimum, corporate contributions and organizational endorsements for key races are frequently paid back with votes. It's here where the machine's potential to do good breaks down, especially when values, issues, and the needs of constituents are traded away for the continued political and financial survival of the machine and its members.

This is where politics gets ugly.

If an elected official continues to play ball, there is always the promise of future machine help in re-election bids. And if an official plays especially well, he or she might be handed an important state party position or even be handpicked to run for higher office, should such a position become available.

Over time, a machine is able to place several of its followers in important positions of power at the local and state government levels as well as at the state party level. Machine control at the state party level means that key machine members can direct party money into important races, and their success can further the power of the machine through patronage and paybacks. Party money can also be earmarked to support or oppose important ballot initiatives that may ensure or threaten the continued existence of the machine. For example, in 1990 the machine decided that millions of dollars in party funds should be directed to fight a term-limits initiative that, if passed, would threaten the continued political careers of key machine members and, thus, the machine itself. So California was stuck with a Republican governor, because Dianne Feinstein had to make do with campaign coffers depleted by a term-limits fight.

The result of all of this is a growing army of machine supporters in various local and state positions of influence. If they oppose the machine or vote independently, they know that their days in office will be numbered. Fear is the controlling force.

A number of candidates new to politics who rely on the machine for funding and support may naïvely believe that once elected, they are free of the machine. They may decide to actually carry out some campaign promises and vote on issues without machine approval. They may even vote against legislation that the machine considers important.

Those politicians are in for the fight of their political lives.

They will find themselves challenged by new candidates at the next election and without political endorsements, campaign finance committees, or contributions. Valued organizational endorsements may also dry up or even appear on an opponent's campaign mailer. Moreover, while still in office, independents may discover that they've been frozen out and isolated, and they may find their own favorite pieces of legislation—no matter how progressive—being opposed by other machine legislators who are following orders. Even in cases where their legislation finally does get passed, they may see key machine members taking the credit.

Over the past several years, I've witnessed how the Burton machine, now largely controlled by Willie Brown, has moved away from supporting passionate issues to a focus on control and power for the sake of control and power. I've also seen how those who play ball are rewarded, and how those who don't are attacked, made to appear ineffective, or exiled from party politics. In this way, good elected officials, who understand the real needs of constituents, often leave office, exhausted by their inability to secure real change and discouraged from trying to do battle on their own.

The Burton machine was the mid-1960s brainchild of Congressman Phil Burton. Burton was first elected to the California State Assembly in the 1950s, and it was there that he began his efforts to build a machine based in San Francisco. In addition to his brother John, whom he was grooming for office, he found a protégé in Willie Brown, John's college friend. In 1964, Phil Burton ran successfully for Congress. The same year, his brother John won a special election for Phil's vacant seat in the assembly. Brown was also elected to the assembly that year.

Through these successes, the Burton machine began to consolidate power in San Francisco and Sacramento, as well as at the state Democratic Party level. In 1973, John Burton became state Democratic Party chairman. By early 1974, Phil Burton, through those loyal to him, was steadily gaining control of the California Democratic Party. This power had spread even further by the end of the year, when John Burton ran for and was elected to Congress, and when several other Burton protégés across California were elected to state offices and to Congress.

One of these men was Art Agnos, a minor political operative. Art's wife and John Burton's wife had become best friends, and when Agnos decided to run for the assembly, he sought Phil Burton's support. John Jacobs, in his book *A Rage for Justice*, suggests that although John Burton had good things to say about Agnos, Phil Burton wasn't convinced and wanted Agnos to meet with him personally for his endorsement. Agnos was coached by machine operatives to promise Burton whatever he asked for.

Agnos went on to win the assembly seat. Although he never became a key member of the Burton machine, his loyalty over the years ensured its support of him for years to come.

The Burton brothers not only came to represent San Francisco in the House of Representatives but, with Phil in command, worked to create a dynasty to ensure the success of their efforts in the future. Their support of their protégés paid off over the years in a number of ways. For example, their support for George Moscone in the 1960s finally gave them control of San Francisco City Hall when, in 1975, Moscone came home from the state senate and put together a new coalition of progressive voters to win the San Francisco mayor's race. This was critical to the machine, as it had been frozen out of city hall politics during the eight years that my dad had been mayor. My dad had refused to play ball with the machine, but he had survived locally thanks to his charisma and political smarts. But Moscone's election in 1975 finally secured for the machine the additional local control that it had wanted.

A year before, in 1974, Phil Burton had rescued Willie Brown from potential exile after Brown had angered Leo McCarthy by unsuccessfully challenging him for the assembly speakership. Brown's failed attempt resulted in McCarthy vindictively stripping him of his power in Sacramento. John Jacobs describes how a well-placed phone call from Phil Burton to McCarthy resulted in new political life for Brown in the form of a key committee chairmanship. The Burtons' long-term support for Brown paid off later, when Brown made his way back up the assembly ranks and, in 1980, finally won the assembly speakership, a position that he held with an iron grip for the next 15 years.

From San Francisco to Sacramento and even to Washington, the Burton machine influenced political decisions through a system of patronage and favors, bestowing the benefits of its power on those who played ball. Initially, the result of all this was the passage of significant legislation in the areas of civil rights, workers' safety and the environment—the effects of which we are still enjoying.

However, the ultimate effect of this massive system of paybacks and favors has been a shift away from a progressive agenda toward one of political power for its own sake. At all levels—local, state, and national—this type of politics has meant that trading of campaign money and endorsements for support for legislation has taken precedence over assessing the quality of that legislation or the needs of constituents. And the machine's original intention of pushing progressive legislation has been replaced by an emphasis on the continued political survival of its leaders. In other words, over the past few years, values have given way to a lust for power.

This degeneration has been damaging to democracy, as voices of dissent and independence continue to be stilled.

These changes probably began in the early to mid-1980s, when total control over the machine moved out of the hands of Phil Burton, and when Phil's original passion for progressive politics gave way to a passion for personal power in the hands of John Burton, Willie Brown, and others. The first sign of these changes was probably in 1982, when John Burton resigned from Congress due to "exhaustion" caused by cocaine and alcohol abuse. Phil Burton started looking for a candidate to run for John's congressional seat, and he asked Art Agnos, whom he'd helped years before. Agnos declined, as he had two small sons and didn't want to commute between Washington and San Francisco. Burton next asked Nancy Pelosi, chair of the state Democratic Party. Pelosi also declined, for similar reasons. Eventually, Marin County Supervisor Barbara Boxer, who had also managed John Burton's Marin County office, sought and received Phil Burton's support.

Another significant change occurred the next year, in 1983, when Phil Burton died suddenly of an aortic aneurysm. His wife Sala immediately announced her intention to run for his seat. There was no party opposition. Sala's brother-in-law John served as her campaign chairman. After resigning from Congress, John had completed a detox program and had begun his slow political comeback by being appointed by Brown to a state commission. Sala won the election, but she died of cancer only three years later. As she lay dying, she handpicked Pelosi to take her seat. Again, there was no party opposition. And once again, John Burton ran the political campaign. Over the next several months, Pelosi won both the primary and the general election.

Other changes were to follow. In 1987, Assemblyman Art Agnos came back to San Francisco and ran successfully for mayor. Agnos's assembly seat was now vacant, and John Burton was ready for the next step in his political comeback. John won the special election and, once again, the two old friends, John and Willie, were fighting side by side in the assembly. In John's next bid for election, after helping Brown fend off a Democratic attack on his speakership, Brown paid Burton back, literally, by raising $70,000 for his re-election campaign. Later, Brown named Burton to chair the assembly's rules committee, a position he had originally held 20 years earlier, before he was elected to Congress. Brown remained Speaker until term limits forced him to seek another elected office in 1995. The one he was finally persuaded to seek was mayor of San Francisco. The next year, term limits also forced John Burton to seek office elsewhere—in the state senate.

I ran against the machine in both elections.

Without Phil Burton, the machine has changed, but its power hasn't lessened. New names have become important at lower levels. In addition to Brown, John Burton and Nancy Pelosi, a rising machine operative concerned mainly with personal power is former San Francisco Supervisor Carole Migden, now in the state assembly. Others dancing cheek to cheek with the machine need not be mentioned here, but they include a number of fearful, rubber-stamp politicians who seemingly need permission to breathe, provide votes when necessary, keep their mouths shut, and stay out of the way.

I wasn't worried about the machine in 1985 when Mitch Fine and Peter Kelly, two top Democratic Party fund-raisers, came to the offices of Alioto & Alioto, the family law office that included my dad, my brothers, and me. The two men offered me the co-chairmanship of the California Democratic Party platform committee. I accepted the appointment immediately. In fact, from 1986 until today, I've been a member of the party's executive board and have rarely missed a meeting during that entire time. I've taken that role seriously. Nevertheless, my first real run-in with the machine came as a result of that co-chairmanship.

There were signs of trouble as early as 1986, when I made my first run for political office as a candidate for the San Francisco Board of Supervisors. I hired a top political consultant who proceeded to orchestrate a nasty and mean-spirited campaign that unfairly targeted Supervisor Wendy Nelder's integrity. Although it was unheard of for a board candidate personally to go after one specific opponent, especially in a large field of candidates, my consultant did just that, working not for my victory but, I think, for Wendy Nelder's defeat. He wasn't successful in either effort.

I've always tried to look only for the good in people. Only recently have I begun to question the motives of others, something I now find distasteful but necessary. At the time, I didn't question the negative campaign tactics that my consultant used against Nelder in my bid for office. After all, I was paying him hundreds of thousands of dollars to do his job, and I figured he must have known what he was doing.

I didn't see this at the time, but looking back, I learned a valuable lesson about the machine's motives. At one point, Joe Mazzola of Local 38, the plumbers' union, one of my dad's closest friends and a great guy, asked me, "What are you doing? Wendy Nelder is it; she's the labor representative on the board." And I naïvely answered, "This is what the consultant told us to do. This consultant wants me to win; we're going to do what he says."

I had no idea what the consultant's bigger picture was, and I had no idea what I was talking about.

The attack was brutal; I didn't even see the mailers used for my campaign. Later I came to realize what was happening. I'll never again participate in or conduct a negative personal campaign.

It seems likely that the machine had designed my campaign as a personal attack against Nelder, who refused to play ball with it. My campaign was likely a political vendetta against her, although I wasn't aware of it. That's how naïve I was about the system.

Wendy Nelder told me later, "The minute you attacked me, I got in the car and drove to see Willie." I believe Brown could have stopped the Nelder attacks, just like that. So it seems obvious that the attack was planned, or at least backed, by Brown. Nelder went to him and he said it was out of his control. But I've learned over the years that nothing in California politics is out of Brown's control— and at this writing, Nelder is working at the office of emergency services, having been hired for the position by Willie Brown.

The result of the 1986 election was that Wendy Nelder narrowly won, coming in fifth place in the field. And up to the day I lost, my consultant was telling me that I was coming in third in all the polls.

Today, my naïveté back then seems almost quaint.

My bid for election served a second purpose as well. The next year, Agnos was elected mayor and I now believe that, in 1986, the machine ran my campaign to help cultivate the city for Agnos. (It's no coincidence that Agnos and I shared the same political consultant.) Machine operatives were able to get all of Joe Alioto's labor people and all of Angela Alioto's progressive support on board for Agnos in 1987. And that's exactly what we did—everything possible for Art Agnos. During his campaign it was a rare day that passed without Agnos calling me, asking me for this, thanking me for that.

But once Agnos took office, the machine no longer needed me. I applied for a seat on the port commission in January 1988, the month Agnos was sworn in as mayor. He had appointed Roger Boas chair of the 50-member committee, and one of his jobs was to review seat recommendations. I received a letter from Boas—who later ran for mayor himself and had some serious legal troubles—turning down my application, saying I was unqualified.

I wasn't unqualified; I was having my first serious brush with the machine. Details do not escape its notice.

This became apparent when I decided to run again for supervisor. I thought that my consultants would return to work on my campaign and that I would have the support of Mayor Art Agnos and my longtime friend, newly elected Congresswoman Nancy Pelosi—the heir to Phil Burton's congressional seat.

But now that their own elections were behind them, it seemed that Agnos and Pelosi no longer needed me or my supporters. They'd both won their races, and it was clear that I was going to be independent of the machine. So the machine, in June 1988, withdrew my consulting team—even though I was clearly going to run. They'd gotten my support and that of my volunteers for the Agnos campaign. The campaigns for the other supervisorial candidates were in high gear. In most instances their finance committees were already in place, collecting funds. I was in trouble, and after thinking things through, I called my friend Kevin Shelley.

The Shelleys and the Aliotos have strong ties to each other. Kevin's father was mayor in the early 1960s, and my father succeeded him. Kevin and I took California Bar review courses together, then the Bar. We were old commiserators.

Kevin told me not to worry, that he'd round up a campaign team for me. He'd been taken advantage of by the Burtons and the Pelosis of the world, and when he saw it happening to me he got upset. He figured he'd hire Michael Ganley and Michael Terris, two top consultants. He said he'd take them out for dinner and buy them a bottle of Bushmills. I had to ask what Bushmills was, but I'll never forget what became known as the "Bushmills meetings"—the beginning of my first successful campaign.

Kevin Shelley considers independent thought a birthright, and the machine frowns on independent thought. I know that I wouldn't be in politics at all if it weren't for Kevin, and I'll never forget—or possibly forgive!—that.

This time the voters showed up. The Alioto name gave me recognition and I had a more professional look—Kevin had suggested I wear my hair up so I wouldn't look like a "screaming banshee." These factors, along with my stand on the issues, won me a seat. Out of 36 candidates vying for six slots, I came in a close second, with Harry Britt—Harvey Milk's heir apparent—becoming president of the board of supervisors.

Art Agnos could pull away his people and prevent them from working on my campaign, but he couldn't manage to renege on their earlier endorsements. Neither could Nancy Pelosi. I won the election with their reluctant support.

In many ways, my own history of fighting the Burton machine in San Francisco parallels my father's experience in running for mayor. Although Dad has told me little over the years about his run-ins with Phil Burton in the 1960s, one story he has shared was about how the machine tried to keep him out of the mayor's office. The machine's candidate, Jack Morrison, was a prop that had been set up to keep Dad from winning the race. The plan was to split the Democratic vote and allow the Republican candidate, Harold Dobbs, to win the mayor's race rather than have an independent-minded candidate like my father gain control of the city.

The plan backfired, however, because of Dad's hard work and broad appeal. After he became mayor, the Burtons vowed they would do whatever they could to hinder him. Hints of mob ties were whispered around town, inspired by the machine's rumor mill.

This is the way machines work.

They sling around innuendo instead of fact, raising doubts in the minds of voters and forcing candidates to spend their resources taking defensive positions. The machine was in large part responsible for ending Dad's ambitions for higher office, but it couldn't get the citizens to turn against him. In his 1971 re-election bid, Joe Alioto won over 70% of the vote, despite the large quantities of mud.

Dad didn't warn me about the machine, partly because his own feud had taken place nearly 20 years before. Phil Burton had now been dead for three years. In an amusing aside, I discovered in my 1996 state senate race against Phil Burton's brother, John, that many voters confused the two Burtons, and after 13 years some still thought that Phil was alive. Worse yet, they told me that they couldn't support me because they were planning to vote for "Phil."

The machine also sets its sights high in targeting enemies.

In 1990, it took a shot at ousting my friend Jerry Brown as California Democratic Party chairman. John Burton called for Jerry's removal, denouncing him as "self-serving, inept, and arrogant" and blaming him for the Democrats' 1990 loss in the races for governor and attorney general. Jerry refused to step down, saying that Burton "just yells and screams and becomes irrational if you don't do exactly what he wants." He also suggested that Burton's criticism of him was unjust because it was Willie Brown and the machine who had chosen to spend over $10 million to fight the California term-limits initiative rather than helping candidates, especially the political campaigns of Dianne Feinstein for governor and San Francisco District Attorney Arlo Smith for attorney general.

John Burton attacked Jerry in front of the party's most dedicated volunteers. People like Burton have never been interested in the grass roots, as Jerry has, but only in preserving their own power and careers. And power and careers would be threatened by passage of the term-limits initiative. The machine wanted to blame Jerry for that—have him take the fall for its own failures and consolidate its own power in the process—so it opposed him for the chairmanship. But even the machine had problems smearing a popular former governor with grassroots support. When it came to a vote, Jerry won, because, unlike the machine, he was close to the people.

Jerry Brown is one of the brightest people I've ever met. He's an intellectual genius, but people often fail to see it. He's always been 20 years ahead of his time. Because of this he's considered a flake by a few people, when he's actually a visionary. Unfortunately, it's not politically advantageous to be a visionary, since that requires stepping on the toes of all those still committed to the old vision. Maybe I identify with Jerry because I draw similar reactions from the powers-that-be. Pass a smoking ban? She's a kook. Fight development of power plants in the area of the world with the highest rate of breast cancer? She's against progress. Do what's right for her poorer constituents? She's crazy.

Jerry is one of those people who got into office because of who he is and because of the ordinary people who support him. The machine can do a lot, but it can't always block grassroots support. Jerry has never focused on spending his time in the corridors of power. He would rather cross the state, meeting with the grass roots of the party—the people who go to party conventions wearing straw hats and hundreds of buttons—and hearing their concerns.

In late 1990, when I refused to sell out Jerry Brown, John Burton took me to breakfast and said, "You know, my friends have been worried about your activities lately."

"John," I replied, "take your best shot, but you better hit me."

The machine has a long memory, and I've been the target of a number of their shots ever since.

Jerry Brown hung on; he withstood the machine's attack. The grass roots of the Democratic Party may not have known what the officials of the party were doing, but they always knew Jerry Brown.

In November 1990, after Jerry had been attacked, the first vice chair of the Democratic Party quit. Jerry and Mitch Fine called me and urged me to run for the position. I agreed, and got on the phone in December to garner support for my election at the upcoming convention in March. For the next several weeks, I spent every day on the phone, and called over 300 executive board members for their endorsements. By January 15, I had the endorsement of 90% of the executive board.

At that point Jerry called again and told me he was not going to run for re-election as state party chair. He had decided to seek the Democratic nomination for president. So Willie Brown and John Burton decided to make Phil Angelides the machine's nominee for state party chair. Then Mitch Fine, who had had me appointed to the state party in 1986, announced his candidacy. I was running unopposed, thanks to the support I had drummed up over the previous six weeks, and once the date to enter the race had passed, I would become the new first vice chair of the party.

When Mitch Fine's election literature was sent out, it included a line saying I endorsed him. Shortly after that, Nancy Pelosi called and asked me to retract my endorsement of Mitch and play ball with the machine —she wanted my support for Phil Angelides. I refused, not only because Mitch is a great friend but because he was eminently qualified for the position.

Then a letter arrived from Pelosi's office, telling me that my executive board membership was being stripped from me. As it turned out, although Mitch Fine had offered me the appointment in 1986, Pelosi was the elected official who had appointment power for the seat that I was given. My appointment in 1986 as co-chair of the party platform committee was to a seat that was Pelosi's to appoint. All Democratic members of Congress and of the state assembly and senate have certain seats they can fill on the state party's executive board. Pelosi was a former state party chair, and she had enormous influence. Although I'd been on the executive board for four years, had almost never missed a meeting, and was running unopposed on the ballot, I'd been unappointed. This unappointment disqualified me from the run for first vice chair.

The plan was to remove me from the executive board, and then fill both my seat and that of the first vice chair after Phil Angelides was elected chair. That way, the machine would be in total control of the party, with Jerry Brown out of the way.

Out of nowhere, I got a call from Nancy Bailey, a party regional director who knew Congressman Jerry Lewis. Lewis's appointment from Southern California had just dropped off the executive board. I'd never met Congressman Lewis, but he was coming to my rescue: The grass roots of the party were apparently outraged that Pelosi had stripped me of my appointment. I flew to Southern California and back to Sacramento to file the appointment papers. Within 24 hours I was back on the executive board, and back in the fight.

The machine rarely loses a battle like that.

In 1991, I won the election as first vice chair, Jerry Brown stepped down to run for the Democratic nomination for president, and Phil Angelides was elected as chair of the state Democratic Party. In my new position I was less vulnerable to the machine, and I was at the height of my popularity in San Francisco. Phil Angelides soon decided to leave his post and run for state treasure. The machine then selected Bill Press to be the party chair.

In early 1996, Bill Press resigned as state Democratic Party chair to take a position with the television program *Crossfire*. Meanwhile, First Vice Chair Arlene Holt, who had been commuting from Washington, D.C., notified the party that she had no interest in moving back to Los Angeles to take Press's position. As second vice chair—the first and second vice chairs switch back and forth between Northern and Southern California—and given the natural line of succession, I should have been able to step up to chair the state Democratic Party. Obviously, there wasn't a chance in hell that

John Burton, Willie Brown, and Nancy Pelosi were going to let that happen. The machine would never give control of the state party to an independent-minded firebrand, as they see me, during an election year. So instead of following the party bylaws, the machine held secret meetings and recruited retired State Senator Art Torres for the position of chair.

I had nothing against Torres—I had even supported him for senator—but when they picked him, they didn't call to ask for my support. Instead, Press called and told me of the meeting after the fact. This would be like Bill Clinton stepping down and telling Al Gore that he was giving the presidency to one of his old friends. I thought about fighting it, because the 3,000 party delegates and the more than 300 members of the executive board didn't know what was going on. I knew I had their support, but in the end I decided to support Torres. I did it for the benefit of the party during an election year in which Clinton needed a strong show of California unity. I don't regret that decision, because I did it out of respect for the grass roots of the party.

One of the things I've seen too often is the negative effect a machine can have on the character of the states and cities of the people it supposedly serves. Although Congressman Phil Burton was a committed environmentalist who helped create the Golden Gate National Recreation Area, which preserved vast lands from development for generations to come, these days the Burton machine subverts any sense of regional heritage.

Growing up here, I was lucky to be able to experience the unique heritage of San Francisco, the colorful neighborhoods, each with its own character, aesthetics, residents, and history. Whether you're walking around Chinatown, the Mission, the Sunset, North Beach, the Marina or the Castro, you can circle the entire world without leaving this great city of Saint Francis.

Too many of my colleagues, both in San Francisco and around the country, worry less about preserving a city and its character than currying the machine's favor. I can't imagine someone like Willie Brown caring much about maintaining this heritage—under his leadership, the state assembly even took away San Francisco's right to create historical landmarks—unless he could increase his own power by doing so.

Although many San Francisco residents have come from somewhere else and may know little about what the city used to be like, they still know what makes the place special. That's why they moved here. They also know that political decisions can't always be made on the basis of dollars alone, and that you don't sell out heritage for a political payback here and a campaign contribution there.

But this sellout of San Francisco is what the machine has been busy doing in recent years. This is what Pelosi has been doing in her efforts to pass legislation to create a trust to manage the Presidio— a trust composed of business interests. And nothing less than an attempted sellout occurred when two former assembly members representing San Francisco worked to help move Giants baseball out of the city. For years I fought hard to ensure that the Giants would remain here. Though there was some limited local opposition, we were eventually successful in getting a ballpark proposition passed by the voters. Before this, however, both John Burton and Willie Brown, supposedly representing the interests of San Francisco, hurt their own city by voting for a law that would have made excess land available for a proposed stadium site in the South Bay. John Burton even contributed some of his own money to the "Yes on G" campaign, which would have built a Giants stadium in San Jose. Though Burton claimed he saw this as the only way to keep the Giants in the Bay Area, there must have been a promise of a vote here, or some political patronage there, and maybe a campaign contribution or a new client in the offing for his private law firm. Whenever I see a particular political action, I question its motives.

Lately I've been wondering how John Burton and Willie Brown both became millionaires while they were supposed to be representing the interests of the city.

With one primary exception in Tom Ammiano, the San Francisco Board of Supervisors has become a rubber stamp for whatever the machine wants. The board members can't stand up for anything as long as they're walking in lockstep with Willie Brown. Even someone like Kevin Shelley, who'd like to make both sides happy, still has to accommodate Brown. Brown's comment, in a recent *New Yorker* article, that the supervisors are "pantywaists" was offensive in its language and its disdain, but there is a certain amount of truth to the assertion—which attests to the power of the machine.

When I studied the First Amendment in law school, I learned about the chilling of free speech. Now I've seen it in action. If Tom Ammiano is the only supervisor to stand up to the mayor and he's going to be drowned out anyway, how much power is that? And how often does this scenario replay itself in local governments all over the country? Debate is necessary in a democracy so that all sides can be heard; and recently there has been little debate in San Francisco, a most politically charged city.

Any government that is run in this manner can lead to a diminishment of freedom. It's never good to chill free speech, stop debate, and remove all forums for healthy dissent. But this is precisely what goes on between a strong executive branch and a rubber-stamp legislative branch, at any level of government. And despite the irony of having a supposedly liberal executive who stifles political forum, the police-state alternative is even more frightening—think of what happened when dissent was suppressed at the Democratic National Convention in 1968 or at Kent State University in 1970.

Midway through Brown's term as mayor, I expect that people will begin to realize that they're suffocating as a result of the chilling of a free exchange of ideas. But how will they fight the machine when they finally wake up? It's one thing to see the effects of machine power; it's another to be able to do something about it.

The public must learn how machine power actually thrives on the first small signs of dissent. As was the case with the Soviet Union in the 1950s and 1960s, quashing dissent when it first appears can actually help machines consolidate power by giving them the opportunity to replace the lone dissenter with another handpicked rubber stamp. If the first one to complain is the first head to roll, then there's little urge to voice a second complaint. Through fear of exile, trivialization, abandonment, and loss of position or campaign funds, the machine has always been successful in preventing the initial stirrings of dissent.

Question authority. Question endorsements. Question attacks. Question fat pocketbooks.

In 1990, the citizens of California, frustrated with career politicians, voted for term limits. The voters liked the idea of ensuring that fresh ideas and new faces would enter the political landscape every six to eight years. A power base takes a long time to build, so term limits would also limit the size of the power base. Not surprisingly, the machine, fearing a loss of influence, pumped millions of dollars of Democratic Party money into fighting Proposition 140, the term-limits initiative—money that could have been better spent electing party candidates to state office. In 1990, the Burton campaign contributed $60,000 of its own money to fight the initiative.

The passage of term limits meant that Burton and Brown both had to leave the assembly in 1996.

But the machine, which exists solely for self-perpetuation, is also a tremendously creative force, and it has managed to turn term limits to its own advantage. Instead of forcing fresh ideas and new faces to enter the political landscape, term limits have opened up new opportunities for the consolidation of machine power. As "old" nonmachine politicians have been forced to leave office, younger machine protégés in various geographical areas have been able to capitalize on the new opportunities to grab political power. Term limits have also created the possibility for a game of political musical chairs. In San Francisco, the machine could put its effort into electing Brown as mayor, moving John Burton to the state senate, and enabling Carole Migden to fill the vacancy left by the departure of a former machine assemblyman—Willie Brown.

In some ways, term limits have instilled yet further loyalty to the machine, because newly elected officials now know that their days in office are literally numbered and that there are many younger politicians waiting in the wings. So a new candidate knows that a future run for office requires that she either create her own system of patronage (always a risky and expensive approach) or follow more closely the dictates of the machine.

Politicians who are in touch with their constituents and the reality of the problems they face can develop a strong power base and stand up to the machine. This has been my approach to public office. For years I worked in the neighborhoods with real people on real issues, attended meetings of citizens' groups, and even did things like take Muni buses to work for six months—I hated every ride, but I was looking for ways to improve the system. An elected official who knows the price of a gallon of milk has a better chance of knowing what her constituents need and deserve. I worked hard and was never afraid to fight for unpopular causes that I knew in my heart were right.

Nevertheless, politics is a game of money. Even a mayor's race now costs millions. Willie Brown, a hypervisible politician in California for over 30 years, had to spend $3 *million* to defeat candidates like Roberta Achtenberg and Frank Jordan and me—candidates who spent maybe a tenth of that amount.

Without money it's more difficult, and sometimes impossible, to win. By controlling major donors and political endorsements, the machine controls the quality of a campaign, because contributions and endorsements mean further financial, group, and volunteer support. This way, the machine has the advantage of control and growth. Continued campaign finance reform may help. We need further legislation to reduce conflicts of interest—both the ties between corporate contributors and future legislation and the private ties between politicians and lobbyists.

To get to the truth about who's behind what, the public must demand to see those things that count in politics: voting records and campaign contribution sources and amounts. Brown can make all the impassioned speeches he wants, but the truth has more to do with contributions from tobacco companies and with votes that favor those companies. Newt Gingrich can call for an end to big government, but a $4 million "book advance" from Rupert Murdoch on the eve of negotiations for the largest telecommunications overhaul in history should tell people a little more.

What's insidious about machine politics is that, by all outward appearances, it seems to be catering to the right causes and doing the right things. In reality, however, machines are destroying real debate about the issues. Machine politics precludes the possibility of balance and fairness, because a machine throws up a barrier to independent, populist politics that cannot be penetrated without permission of the machine itself. Your political views may or may not jibe with those of someone like Ross Perot or Pat Buchanan or Jerry Brown, but those views should be heard by the people.

Machines forbid that.

Ross Perot may have a billion dollars to throw into a campaign, but the machines will bar him from debates and deny him endorsements, relegating him to the sidelines. Pat Buchanan hurls accusations at big business, and the Republican machine keeps him out of the Big Tent. Jerry Brown may have sensible ideas for returning government to the people who need it, but he's too far to the left for the Democratic machine to tolerate. The machines conspire to leave independent-minded candidates out in the cold.

At all levels—local, state and national—free speech and the free exchange of ideas is being chilled to the freezing point. And machines at all levels prefer it that way. Our only hope for bypassing this autocracy is to be educated and to take with a grain of salt everything but the unassailable facts.

THE HERETICS:
WOMEN IN POLITICS

Fiercely were they
Adverse to me, my party, and the blood
From whence I sprang.

INFERNO, CANTO X

WHEN DANTE AND HIS GUIDE VIRGIL enter the city of Satan in the sixth circle of Hell, you know that the really awful stuff has begun. The heretics live in unsealed tombs dotting the ground inside the city walls, and there are red-hot towers tipped with flames. It is misty and difficult to see or breathe. Our childhood ideas of Hell, with its pitchfork-waving devils and fire and brimstone, come from this canto of the *Inferno*. The inhabitants of this part of Hell are the people who in life were devoted to evil.

Dante, living in a certain time and place, naturally and understandably held certain attitudes. Though most of these attitudes were universally accepted in his day, some of them are no longer considered valid, and many are offensive to us. In particular, Dante's perspective on women reflected the views of his age. Harpies and she-wolves, creatures who pose a danger to men's souls, populate his landscape of Hell.

These days, of course, we don't use women to symbolize universal faults of character. But a look at women in politics at the end of the twentieth century might make a contemporary reader more forgiving of Dante's anger and mistrust of women.

This is the hardest thing I've ever written, but my story of politics—the underlying story—can't be told without it.

How can I possibly denigrate so many women like this, calling them heretics? How can this be taken as anything other than sour grapes? So I didn't get the political backing I needed, and I lost. If a women's group chooses to endorse another candidate over me, I should take my lumps and refuse to cry over spilt milk, right? If my women colleagues decide that a different candidate—a man—is better qualified for a position than I am, well, that's the game.

I don't accept that.

Plenty of people who read this book will be keeping a sharp eye out for what looks like whining, or denunciations of a process that didn't serve me personally, or complaints that my first eight years of public service have drawn to a close.

Look no further. People will point to this section as negative. As vindictive. As destructive. But it's not intended to be any of those things. It's an unapologetic look at how our system fails not just one candidate, but many. It's a condemnation of a political system that fails half of our country's citizens: women.

Women have made and will keep making significant, deep inroads in the political landscape. Anne Richards, the powerful Democratic former governor of Texas, advanced women's causes just by getting elected to govern that state. U.S. Representative Maxine Waters has fought hard for her constituents in Los Angeles, and for all Americans, by championing racial equality at the congressional level. Roberta Achtenberg was the first openly gay person to serve at the highest levels of a presidential administration. President Bill Clinton appointed her to the Department of Housing and Urban Development, and she stared down the most reactionary members of the Senate—including the formidable and frightening Jesse Helms—to win confirmation. She later waged a brave political battle to become mayor of San Francisco, and it took the concerted efforts of the California Democratic machine to stop her.

Women like these are examples to everyone, men and women alike, of what politics ought to be. They are women who fight for what's important to all of us, but bring a particular passion to issues that are crucial to women—issues of nonviolence, the right to choose, and tolerance. They are examples of how women, by pooling their political strength, can make a difference in government.

We've come far. But we have a daunting distance yet to go.

In March 1996, during my race against John Burton for California State Senate, I went to the *San Francisco Examiner* building for an interview about my campaign. Journalist Stephanie Salter handed me a mailer that Burton had just sent out to women voters. She then asked, "How do you feel about your colleagues now?"

I hadn't yet seen the mailer. On the front page was a photo of John Burton and the words: "As we choose between John Burton and Angela Alioto for state senate. . .here's what women have to say about John Burton." Inside were the faces of 26 women, all political officeholders. They were in two groups. On the left, above the photos and names of 17 women, a caption read, "Here's what the women who work with John Burton say about John Burton." Among these names were several state assemblywomen, state senators, and others, including Congresswoman Nancy Pelosi. On the right side, above the photos and names of nine other women, was another caption that read, "Here's what the women who work with Angela Alioto say about John Burton." This group included all of my fellow women on the San Francisco Board of Supervisors, as well as San Francisco City Attorney Louise Renne. On the back page were photos of U.S. Senators Barbara Boxer and Dianne Feinstein. Congresswoman Lynn Woolsey, a strong supporter of mine who had wanted to endorse me, must have come under a tremendous amount of pressure to appear in the piece. None of the women quoted in the Burton mailer attacked me directly, but their silence about me spoke as loudly as their support for John Burton.

I was visibly shaken by this piece of campaign literature. Stephanie Salter saw this and wrote a piece entitled "It Broke the Heart of San Francisco"—a play on my 1992 campaign slogan, "The Heart of San Francisco."

When the mailer reached the mailboxes of women around San Francisco, the calls began to come in. Young women asked, "What's wrong with Angela that her colleagues would do this to her?" Not one asked, "What's wrong with her colleagues?" But to me, it was the latter question that needed an answer.

Over the previous several years I'd experienced firsthand the power of the political machine. My problem was that I'd never wanted to play the game. I knew the rules, but as Mario Cuomo said in explaining his unsuccessful campaign for the governorship of New York, I had no desire to sell my own soul for political advancement and survival.

Women know how the game is played—or they're not invited to the game. Over the years I've seen many women who were willing to do whatever it took to get ahead, even if it meant selling out other women. This willingness is far more disturbing than the actions of sexist politicians like Willie Brown or John Burton, because it reveals the lack of real power in the hands of women politicians in America. It tells me that there are many women in politics who only give off the appearance of political independence. It says to me that women have a long way to go to truly achieve the freedom to stand up for real women's issues—independent of male-dominated political machines. As long as political parties at the national, state, and local levels continue to be dominated by power brokers who care less about issues than consolidating power, true political reform and the responsible use of power by women for women will remain a distant dream.

As an instrument of the political machine, Congresswoman Nancy Pelosi had me removed from my position in the California Democratic Party for refusing to endorse the machine's candidate for party chair, Phil Angelides. She was in the forefront of attacks against me for my longtime support of my friend Jerry Brown. Yet before I went against the machine, thereby threatening her own position, I'd always considered Pelosi a friend.

Growing up, my daughter Angela Mia's best friend was Pelosi's daughter Alexandra. When I decided to run for supervisor in 1986, Pelosi served as my finance chair. I couldn't have been more in her debt, and she told me she admired my courage in running for public office. Her father and brother had both served as mayor of Baltimore, and her father also had been in Congress. We had a lot in common.

One day in 1987, after Sala Burton had handpicked her to take over her seat in Congress, Pelosi came by the house. She was distraught because she had just learned that Dianne Feinstein might be thinking about running for the seat, and she was concerned about an ugly campaign between the two of them. As it turned out, however, Feinstein had no plans to oppose Pelosi that year, so Pelosi ran against Harry Britt, and she won.

I walked neighborhoods and campaigned hard for Pelosi. The next year, after she was elected, I expected Pelosi to help me in my own campaign as I'd helped her. I thought we were on the same team. And although I received her early endorsement, by late 1988 I was being frozen out. The situation worsened as it became obvious that I was more interested in the issues and less concerned about paying homage to the machine.

The direction Pelosi chose in our relationship saddened me; we should have been natural allies. I had gone out on a limb in supporting her against Harry Britt, who represented the gay community. But I did so because of our friendship and because she was a woman. Unfortunately, I hadn't anticipated the strength of her political nature and her ambition. She no longer seems like the woman who had high hopes for a progressive, pro-woman agenda; she's now, unfortunately, just a cog in the machine.

When I saw Pelosi's name and photo in the Burton mailer, I wasn't surprised. Pelosi had long before shown me where she placed her loyalties; it wasn't in friendship, and it certainly wasn't in helping elect another woman to public office.

To what extent will some women sell out their own to further their political careers and their relationships with the machine? Several political women, including California State Assemblywoman Carole Migden and U.S. Senator Barbara Boxer, have emerged against logic and their own good judgment on the wrong side of a particularly nasty scandal in Sacramento.

The Connolly affair was first made public in San Francisco in the late summer of 1995, when I was running for mayor of San Francisco. At that time, two young women, Meredith Anderson and Lori Arbogast, came to San Francisco with their attorney, Cathryn Chinn, to discuss their accusations of sexual harassment by their boss, Democratic State Assemblyman Tom Connolly. They'd both been fired after complaining about the harassment and were personally devastated. Initially, they had voiced their complaints quietly, and then-assembly Speaker Willie Brown and Rules Committee Chairman John Burton had hired attorney Nina Ryan to investigate the charges.

Ryan conducted a large-scale investigation that produced a mass of evidence, which she condensed into a short executive summary. She found, officially, that the two women were lying. When the women sued the state, however, the other evidence, which had been officially disregarded by Brown, Burton and Ryan, came to light. Among the many newly surfaced facts were testimony from witnesses supporting the women—and documents that showed Brown instructed Nina Ryan to withhold evidence during the legislative investigation.

When this cover-up was discovered and hit the media, Brown called out his troops. Carole Migden and Barbara Boxer—who had fought fiercely against Senator Bob Packwood in his sexual harrassment scandal—and the other women of the machine came to Brown's support. Even Gloria Steinem wrote a letter in his defense. Nevertheless, things looked bad for Brown.

In any other state, the career of the Speaker of the state legislature would have come crashing down in the face of a cover-up like this. Willie Brown is blessed, however, with an uncanny sense of timing, a knack for deflecting criticism, and more than his share of good luck. As the scandal was beginning to take off and it looked like Brown might end up in the hot seat, a strange and wonderful thing happened on the way to city hall. Brown's opponent in the runoff race for San Francisco mayor, incumbent Frank Jordan, decided, as a publicity stunt, to take an on-the-air shower with a couple of Los Angeles radio disc jockeys. Someone brought a camera, and the next day the mayor's face—and nude body—was spread across the front pages of San Francisco's two newspapers. Here was the conservative mayor and former police chief, naked, with these two men. Immediately, the debates left Willie Brown and sexual harassment in the dust to concentrate on the crucial matter of Jordan's shower—which, by the way, I have strong suspicions about, since Jordan is not a stupid man, and he must have known that the stunt would have cost him the mayorship. I've had a lot of interesting discussions with friends about why he really did it.

In any event, all the controversy surrounding Brown's sexual harassment cover-up disappeared from the press—and from the important mayoral debate that night. Its disappearance enabled Brown to hold onto another remarkable coup: he had earlier obtained the support of two major women's organizations over his two women opponents.

It's not easy for a woman to run for political office in America. In order to take a stab at it, she has to make her way up through the ranks of local political groups to become known in the community, seek grassroots support, raise money, and secure key endorsements.

It is in this last area that women have traditionally run into brick walls. Without endorsements it is nearly impossible to secure the added support and money required to run an effective campaign, and political machines at the local, state and national levels are designed to help the campaigns of men before they help women.

Women's organizations have traditionally played a vital role in securing endorsements for women candidates. They serve to help educate average women—working women, soccer moms—about which candidates will work on their behalf. Across the country, local chapters of the National Organization for Women (NOW) and the National Women's Political Caucus (NWPC) fulfil this role. In many instances, they've helped previously unknown women candidates attain the visibility required to secure the funds and grassroots support they need. Recently, however, local and state chapters have begun hitching their wagons to candidates that at best gloss over or ignore issues important to women and at worst are actively hostile to women—the League of Women Voters, for instance, endorsed Ronald Reagan for president, despite his opposition to the Equal Rights Amendment.

In the 1995 San Francisco mayoral race, Roberta Achtenberg and I wrote a joint letter to the local NOW chapter and asked for a joint endorsement. We made this request at the same time that the Brown–Burton harassment cover-up scandal was establishing a toehold in the press. In light of the developing legislative sleaze, we expected an automatic endorsement. After all, NOW had been established to fight for women's rights, one of which is the right to work in an environment free of sexual harassment and protected from sexual discrimination.

Not only did the local NOW chapter refuse to endorse me, but they also refused to endorse Achtenberg, a lesbian activist whose entire political career has focused on women's rights. Instead, NOW openly endorsed what they called a pro-feminist male candidate, Willie Brown, even though this "feminist" had done everything he could to cover up a politically devastating case of sexual harassment during his watch at the state capitol. (This made me wonder what exactly a "feminist" man was.) A few months later, in my 1996 California State Senate race against John Burton, the local chapter of the NWPC took the position of refusing to endorse *any* candidate.

Sour grapes on my part, maybe. Yet if I am angry, it's not just because of the way Achtenberg and I were treated. It is because these organizations represent themselves as possessing integrity and caring about advancing women's political causes. But when a group like the NWPC withholds its endorsement from a qualified woman candidate running against a man, something is clearly wrong with the endorsing organization.

The NWPC has three local chapters—in San Francisco, Marin, and Sonoma. As a man, John Burton was prohibited from appearing before the NWPC's endorsement committees or from being endorsed. Nevertheless, perhaps by some act of magic, he was able to secure the names of all the committee members—something no one is officially allowed to do. While I was called before the three NWPC committees for three different interviews to solicit their support, John Burton wrote each member individually, seeking a decision of "no endorsement" in the campaign. The San Francisco and Marin chapters obliged him and the political machine. To their credit, the Sonoma chapter defected; they endorsed me and told the other chapters that they were out of their minds. Soon after, I received a call from NWPC's state president. She was distressed and told me that she would move to discredit the local chapters for violating their charter. But the bottom line was that these chapters had effectively come out for a man—moreover, a man unfriendly to both women's issues and women themselves.

Burton won the election.

What does this kind of political action (and inaction) tell women voters? Think of a reasonably well-educated, politically active woman voter. She probably has a job and, more likely than not, children and a house to look after and a million other worries. She wants to stay informed, and she knows what issues are important to her as a woman, but she doesn't have time to read every newspaper article, attend every speech, and pore over every editorial that mentions the candidates.

This woman, and the millions like her, is the target of women's political organizations. She's going to vote, she's independent-minded (not content merely to vote with her husband or father), and her main source of information is endorsement flyers. There's a reason that every candidate mails out tens of thousands of these, even in local races: people rely on them for their information.

What does the San Francisco career woman, or the NYU student active in progressive politics, or the working mother in Mississippi struggling to get by think when she opens her mail and sees NOW's slate card endorsing the leading male candidate? That NOW is cynically endorsing the politician who is more likely to win, thereby currying his favor? More likely, she'll suspect that the women candidates are less competent, less qualified, and less able to lead than the man. The fact that the slate card is rife with the photos of women climbing on board in support of this endorsement will be further incentive for her to climb aboard too.

Beneath this, however, there's an even deeper message being communicated, and that is that men are still inherently better, *more fit* for public office than women. Actions such as those by the local NOW and NWPC chapters do more than merely validate the candidacy of men like Willie Brown and John Burton. These actions may well serve to *invalidate* the political lives and opinions of women—especially women depending on endorsements to level the political playing field—and move them even farther away from politics. My fear is that machine strategies may inhibit the movement of conscientious women into politics at any level. An attitude of "Why run if my male opponent is going to be judged as better?" or worse still, Why run against a superior, male candidate?" is eventually going to develop, and that will be devastating not simply for women, or for politics, but for everybody.

The truth behind women's organizations' endorsements is simple, of course—as simple as anything else in politics.

Shortly after Brown took office as mayor, and immediately after the primary election of John Burton to the California State Senate, Anna Shimko, the head of the local chapter of the NWPC, was appointed as a salaried commissioner of the City and County of San Francisco. Andrea Shorter, of the local chapter of NOW, was appointed to a vacant salaried elected position on the community college board.

Can it be that women's organizations, founded specifically to advance the cause of women's politics and, ultimately, the welfare and rights of women nationally, have abandoned their lofty principles and sold themselves to the highest bidder? That many women who acquire political power are no more than cogs in the machine, and that an endorsement from NOW implies political paybacks and backroom deals?

And that independent women candidates, out to buck the system and try to make a real difference, are on their own?

Meet Daddy's Little Girl.

If a woman decides to enter the political arena, she better either have a thick skin already, or grow one quickly. When I first decided I would scale back a lucrative career in law to run for public office,

I had two distinct advantages: terrific name recognition and sufficient money. I'm a woman, though, and both of these factors, which would have assured an easy ride for a man, were turned viciously against me. I was seen as a threat to the status quo.

In 1986 I was labeled "Daddy's Little Girl," a sexist epithet that offends on a number of levels. I was, by implication, riding on Joe Alioto's coattails and spending his money—a spoiled brat who got everything she wanted. My opponents, bankrolled and fed their material by the machine, gleefully trotted this line out at every opportunity. Even my fellow women candidates didn't seem offended by the implications.

The fact is my father and I have fundamental differences and many similarities. I've never been anything other than proud of him, but sometimes I had to focus on our differences to make my political voice heard.

The "Daddy's Little Girl" tag speaks volumes about the state of politics in this country. In a two-second sound bite we can reduce a candidate to a mere thing, a puppet, an impotent shadow candidate—and this is often done by politicians who are themselves puppets of the machine. And this particular tag resonates with voters; we are conditioned to accept such a label. It's easier to believe that a woman has no voice of her own, that she is taking her cues from some smarter and more capable source (a man), than it is to accept the fact that a woman candidate is every bit as valid, and vital to the political system, as a man is—at times even more so. The lack of public outcry over such a label points to society's complicity in condoning this kind of thinking, and is the source of a tremendous obstacle in achieving equality for women.

The personal lives of women politicians and political candidates are fair game, much more so than they are for men. Unless a man engages in a blatant indiscretion (we can ask Gary Hart about this), his personal life is generally not of much interest. But women are held to a different standard: they are judged by the quality of the men in their lives. Michael Dukakis's wife has a problem with alcohol addiction? She spends time in a clinic and is hailed for her courage; it doesn't reflect on Michael. Hillary Clinton, pilloried in the media for any number of scandals, nonetheless did not detract a whit from her husband's popularity in polls conducted throughout 1996. Yet let Enid Waldholtz's husband write bad checks and rip off his family—she's no longer the congresswoman from Utah. If a woman politician, at a local level, tries to have a social life, she better be careful about not only her own actions and activities, but those of her friends and associates.

According to the standards by which we judge women, a woman's worth is a direct reflection of the men in her life. What does her husband do for a living? What is her father up to these days? And the important, unasked question: Which of these men is the *real* influence in her political voice?

It is rare that the media and the public hold a man up to the same scrutiny. Their wives and mothers and girlfriends either "know their places" and therefore are not a bad influence on the candidate or politician, or are loose cannons—independent-minded, that is—yet somehow don't reflect badly on the man in question.

The machine is well aware of this double standard and uses it to great effect. In 1991 Herb Caen reported that a man I had seen socially, Rusty Arcias, was the new "love of my life." During the 1995 mayoral race in San Francisco, Willie Brown solicited Areias's endorsement and invoked his name in public against me, saying Rusty had told him I was "crazy."

It must be true, if some man says it is.

When Brown is seen dating woman after woman, the press is naturally interested, but no scandal erupts. Yet imagine a woman candidate or politician seen out at a social event with a man on each arm, laughing and winking.

You think that woman candidate would be able to spend one more day in politics?

This double standard adds to a woman politician's liability. Unlike men, women politicians need to remain scrupulously above any hint of scandal. In many ways, they need to be better politicians than men, since they are under closer scrutiny. There's no room for a false step. This is not an easy task for anyone, and it's especially difficult in a society already hostile to ambitious women. Unfortunately, these conditions drive women politicians away from serving the larger interests of women by hardening them, and encourages alliances with the machine for self-protection and their own personal power—and those alliances soon write the script they're to follow, sometimes eagerly.

This is additionally unfortunate because women have the capability of seeing the world in a different way than men do, and of using these insights to bring substantive change to government.

No matter how hard we try to ignore gender, differences between men and women do exist and are in fact crucial to America's political health. Men and women have different qualities and viewpoints that can affect them both as voters and as public officials. Even with the significant cultural changes of recent decades, the historical role of women as primary caregivers has not changed. Whether or not they work outside of the home, women are the primary providers of both child care and elder care in our society. If married, women are typically responsible for determining how child care is arranged. If a sick child needs care at home, more often than not it's the mother who fills this role, even if she has her own career. Moreover, women live longer and—far more often than men—are those who care for their dying spouses and parents.

Women often are fulfilling these responsibilities as they also attempt to establish their own careers. While a few seek careers as a way to utilize all of their talents, most do so out of necessity, all the while trying to balance their needs at work with the welfare of their families.

I know the personal conflicts, choices, and tragedies they can face along the way. I attended law school against my husband's wishes and raised a family. Between law school, motherhood, my first law firm job and studying for the California Bar, I obviously had a full plate. Yet what I went through isn't much different from the obstacles that any woman with a family and a career faces. Women are, given their role in society, intimate with matters of family, caring for the sick, the special problems of women, and issues of child care, health, and family leave.

Perhaps as a result of the experience of being a woman in this country, perhaps because of this caregiving role, many women see the problems of society differently than men do. This doesn't mean that women's viewpoints are better than men's (does it?); it just means that women have viewpoints that reflect the knowledge they've gained from their unique experiences.

Women make up over 50% of the American population, but their view of society is seldom mirrored in how our laws are written. This isn't because women's ideas are deliberately ignored, but because men generally think about such issues from their own perspectives.

I chaired the San Francisco Board of Supervisors' Health Committee for six years. Many of the members were men who agreed with me on most issues, including RU486 legislation and a number of other issues of particular importance to women. Indeed, men like former governor Jerry Brown are certainly sympathetic to women and women's issues. They go out of their way to try to understand the importance of a compassionate agenda that places emphasis on items of special importance to women, and in many areas they should be considered leaders in promoting women's legislation. But they don't have the same intimacy with those issues that women do.

Women's special perspective is one of the most critical reasons why they must become even more politically aware and active. Their awareness of policies affecting women *in particular* allows them to raise issues that men don't think about. These include general health concerns, which range from health care to environmental protection. For instance, much of the national legislation for school retrofitting to remove asbestos and lead-based paint has been introduced by women lawmakers. I believe the reason for this is that women see the link between a healthy environment and healthy children. Women know that environmental issues affect the health of children and, therefore, the quality of family life.

In this regard, women—especially mothers—know that there are two economic bottom lines. The first is the immediate economic concern related to increased costs of services or loss of jobs. Women support themselves financially in great numbers and actually outnumber men in the workforce, and often are the sole providers for their children. They worry about the costs of housing, child care, and basic sustenance.

But more important, women are also keenly aware of the long-term costs of ignoring environmental and health concerns. They understand that there is a second bottom line related to future economic and health costs to their children. It's no coincidence that far more women than men have testified at my committee hearings on environmental and health issues. They know that a cost savings now should never be made at the expense of the health of the population tomorrow.

Men often overlook this crucial aspect of our economy.

When Pacific Bell sought approval to place cell phone antennas, housed in black boxes, throughout San Francisco's neighborhoods, the board of supervisors was ready to agree without much debate. The city would benefit financially from fees paid by Pacific Bell, and Pacific Bell would prosper and provide more jobs and services. It looked, at first glance, like a win-win situation.

I and a number of other women voiced concern over the potential health risks associated with cell phone antennas. They may be a source of potentially carcinogenic emissions that can also suppress the immune systems of some people, such as those who are HIV-positive. I never had any intention of stopping progress, but a plan was needed before any additional boxes were placed in the city. Pac Bell would be only the first communication company to request the right to place such boxes. Obviously, competing companies would soon get into the act, resulting in a huge number of antennas in San Francisco—and across the country. Women needed questions about the process answered.

After I aired these health concerns, I discovered a morass of regulations that actively discount the health issue of antenna placement. Why? Because it is not the type of concern that men in positions of corporate authority—who are interested in short-term profits—would ever take into consideration. Similarly, such concerns are rarely raised by men in positions of political power—immediate economic advantages are of far more concern to them as a rule. Thus, the humongous telecommunications law passed by Congress and signed by President Clinton—and authored, in large part, by industry lobbyists—explicitly states that health concerns need not be taken into consideration in the permit process for cellular antennas. That is unconscionable.

If there's any possible health risk associated with transmitter boxes, I don't want them near my children or anyone else's children. The rest of the board heard this argument and voted to continue the hearings. We all agreed to discuss the matter. But the law was clear, and the billions that the industry was worth spoke louder than a few women concerned about cancer in their neighborhoods.

After the hearings I received a letter from a young mother, Mary Irene Zemanic, who had attended the hearings with her daughters, Alex and Lorrin. She wrote that she hoped her daughters would grow up with a sense of perseverance and an understanding of their potential to affect their political environment in some good way. I was gratified that Mary used my commitment to a health issue as an example to them.

This was more than mere fan mail. It's the reason I stepped into the Hell of politics in the first place—so that Alex and Lorrin might have a better future. It's also significant that Mary and her daughters were the ones who wrote me, since this issue, like all issues related to health and environment, is of special significance to women. Mary's letter suggests that more and more women are understanding this fact explicitly, that they are thinking about it. An issue as esoteric and convoluted as cell phone antenna placement is the kind of issue that is going to loom large in the future, just as the smoking issue has begun to do. In the end, male-dominated thinking —and lobbying—are going to take a backseat to the deeper aspects of these issues.

In 1996, women activists from the predominantly working-class African American neighborhood of Bayview–Hunter's Point asked me to write legislation to prevent the city from building a *third* power plant in the neighborhood. The legislation passed strongly— proof of the power women can wield when they unite. The immediate economics of the issue, which seemed to guarantee approval, were deflected by a grassroots campaign of educating men and women to the fact that women in Hunter's Point, an area that already had two power plants, have the highest rates of breast and cervical cancer in San Francisco—a city that has one of the highest rates of breast cancer in the industrialized world. This education led to demonstrations and a show of public disapproval, which in turn brought about the demise of the project.

Together, men and women can create a balance that's invaluable for finding solutions to social problems. Men can't do it alone; neither can women. Instead, it takes full representation, by both men and women, to obtain a broader perspective. In this way, women have something powerful to offer to politics, government, and society, both as individuals and by virtue of their being women.

In the parlance of the Roman Catholic Church, a heretic is a person who denies the doctrine of the church, who fails to recognize the importance of the integrity of the structure of the church. Dante recognized the danger of heretical action and beliefs. Heretical action was not simply exercising freedom of thought, it was a deliberate and selfish attempt to gain salvation, to betray the welfare of the many for personal gain.

Women put themselves into a parallel heretical position by speaking out against other women for selfish political reasons. After all, there is far more at stake in politics than the advancement of women's issues, or even the achievement by women of a distinct and powerful voice. The survival of our society depends on the political equality of women.

At what point is America going to become a wasteland of cancerous agents, of an abysmal live birthrate—already the lowest among all industrialized nations—and of children going without lunch at school because wealthy corporations aren't made to pay their fair share of taxes?

We are already more than halfway there.

Women must make the difference. It is vital for women to support political women who lay aside the traditional lure of politics —personal power and material gain—in favor of the reason women got into politics in the first place: to make a difference in women's lives, and therefore in the lives of all Americans.

Women have a poor record of supporting women candidates in America over the last 25 years. Yet to effect any substantive changes in government, women need to stick together. As candidates and politicians, they must support other women running for office and do what they can to ensure their victory. To accomplish this, they must see themselves first and foremost *as women*, with visionary political agendas, independent voices, and a unique and vital perspective on issues that affect all of us. To sell out to the machine for personal gain is to betray not merely their fellow women candidates, but the spirit of the Constitution—a spirit we would all like to believe exists out there somewhere—and our society as a whole.

As voters, women need to understand that they too have a responsibility to seek this balance. Women must look beyond the pettiness of political campaigns, of questionable agendas by organizations and meaningless sound bites that focus on a woman candidate's hairstyle or cookie recipes. *Women must elect women.* Men will not elect women: that has been proven throughout the history of this country.

We must see beyond the attacks on women candidates and politicians, which are the main cause of the lack of advancement by women in politics—not inability or incompetence. The fact that many of these attacks are carried out by women must not cloud the reality: it is in the machine's interest *only* that progressive, pro-women candidates are kept silent. What else can explain why Hillary Clinton's most vociferous attackers are women, despite her high approval rating by women in the general populace?

To seek true equality, to address specific *wrongs* as well as less obvious ills, women must recognize their perspective and potential. They must rise above the political infighting that characterizes them to such an unpleasant degree. They must show how broader women's issues affect everyone. They must have a vision for the future in which they play an invaluable and *equal* part. They must allow themselves political power.

Alex and Lorrin are depending on it.

THE VIOLENT:
REAL AND IMAGINARY
CRIME AND CRIMINALS

Oh, foolish wrath! who so dost goad us on
In the brief life, and in the eternal then
Thus miserably overwhelm us.

INFERNO, CANTO XII

A MONG THOSE DANTE MEETS in the seventh circle of Hell are those who brought harm to others during their lives. Dante, living in the dangerous time and place he did, was understandably concerned that the violent should be suitably punished—a concern that we share in America, especially as we approach the next century in a society that breeds violence and glorifies the instruments of harm. No sensible person would argue that a violent criminal ought to be anywhere except locked up.

In addition to violent criminals, however, this circle of Hell might also hold a place for those who commit violence against America's soul, who scapegoat people who can't fight back. One problem with American politics is that our leaders—men like Jesse Helms, Newt Gingrich, Pete Wilson, and many other politicians in both parties—insist on selling the public a high-profile, mean-spirited, politicized public-safety agenda that draws attention away from real crime and its causes. It also creates a group of criminals where there wasn't one before.

We can see this clearly in the efforts of some political leaders to "fight" homelessness, to target youth as potential criminals, and to call for large-scale police action without justification. By focusing on *imaginary* crimes and criminals, these politicians take public attention and resources away from finding real solutions to our problems, and from fighting real crime and criminals. In many ways these political leaders perpetuate policies that make real violence much more possible, compounding their own crime of scapegoating others.

We are all familiar with the stereotype of thousands of potentially productive Americans sitting on our city sidewalks, panhandling near cash machines, setting up tent cities in our parks, or using welfare or SSI benefits to support alcoholism or drug addiction. But the problems of poverty and homelessness extend far beyond the stereotypes created by politicians and the media.

When I decided to tackle these problems as a San Francisco supervisor, I started with a question, one people rarely ask: Who are the homeless? A recent study conducted by a San Francisco research consulting firm found that 77% of homeless people are disabled in one or more ways. Of these, 59% have psychiatric conditions, and over two-thirds have abuse problems with alcohol, drugs, or both. Another study found that one-third of homeless people are infected with tuberculosis, and more than one in ten are infected with HIV. Most of these people are unaware of their health status.

Estimates of the numbers of homeless people who are also veterans range as high as 40%. Bernie is a homeless man who served 18 years in the Navy. He often stands outside city hall, making airplanes out of aluminum soda cans. I've bought his planes from time to time, and he has sent them to me at Christmas. The Navy, he told me once, taught him how to "double fist"—that is, to down two drinks at a time, holding one in each hand. He said by the time he got out of the service, he was an alcoholic. He spent all his money on liquor. The homeless population includes thousands of people like Bernie, who leave a regimented, disciplined system—like the Navy—unprepared to deal with the outside world. Of course, neither the military nor the Veterans Administration has done much to help homeless veterans. Activist local governments, with state and national support, are going to have to pound out solutions.

The largest increase in the homeless population in recent years has been among women and children. Among the homeless women

I've met is Sharon, a woman in her twenties with two small children. She is intelligent and attractive and has never used drugs. She, her husband, and their two children used to live in a nice home in an upper-middle-class San Francisco neighborhood. When Sharon's husband ran out, she had no family to turn to and, unable to pay the rent, she was forced to move into a shelter in Polk Gulch, the city's notorious red-light district. During the day she is on the streets and at night she and her children live on the top floor, fearful of the other residents—some of whom are criminals and many of whom are drug and alcohol abusers. Sharon and her children live in constant fear, yet she has accepted this life in order to feed her children without turning to prostitution. And Sharon is one of the resolute ones. Many women like her have even fewer choices and do whatever is necessary to feed their children.

There are thousands of women like Sharon—alone with their children, no job, and no skills. None of us see ourselves as at risk for ending up in a shelter—or worse—but the fact is that homeless people come from somewhere, and sometimes it's from nice homes that have been abandoned by the husband. Men are not immune, either. The uneducated and unskilled—but still employable—are always in danger of being put out in the street. Contrary to popular opinion, government unemployment benefits are neither endless nor generous. And once someone is on the street, especially if they have known the comfortable middle class all their lives, they are statistically likely to become drug-dependent, alcohol-dependent, or mentally ill, with the possibility of such a fate increasing with the amount of time they are homeless. If you think you're immune, spend just a few minutes wandering around the poorest section of town, imagining losing not just everything you own, but your plans and dreams for your future and your kids' futures.

This is who the homeless are. They are Americans who had a dream at one time, who contributed to the economy, or served to defend their country, or cooked meals for their children and got them on the bus to school—or they are children who were in school once. They are people.

Elected officials could prevent the plight of women like Sharon from ever occurring by recognizing the importance of not allowing people to find themselves on the streets in the first place. Once a person is there and goes looking for help, she's the one we need to take care of immediately, especially since the success rate is so great. Our government ought to see to it that everyone is well protected in emergency situations. *Welfare* is not always a dirty word, and people like Sharon would be far better off with some minimal guarantees, such as continued medical insurance and the promise of food and a safe place to live while they get their lives back in shape.

Nevertheless, in recent years San Francisco and other American cities have taken a reactionary approach that ensures people will end up on the street—and makes it harder for them to leave the street.

Most politicians' answer to the question of what to do with homeless people is to create a hostile environment and drive them to more remote neighborhoods. Yet this merely masks the problem rather than solving it. In 1993, San Francisco Mayor Frank Jordan initiated "Matrix," ostensibly a program to eliminate homelessness, but really a method of getting panhandlers off shopping-district sidewalks. These new imaginary criminals could be arrested for blocking a doorway, sleeping between the hours of 10:00 P.M. and 6:00 A.M., or even carrying a cardboard box—a particularly ridiculous criminal designation known as "encampment." Under this program, many citations were issued to homeless people for urinating in public—long before San Francisco signed a deal with JCDecaux to place public toilets around town, and at a time when the few public toilets that existed in Golden Gate Park were locked to keep out "junkies." My friend Alex Bennett drew attention to this inexplicable practice and worked hard to change the policy.

Imagine the humiliation and anguish of first being in a position in which you have to relieve yourself in public, and then being arrested for doing so. People don't urinate in public because they want to, but because they have to. One day, on my way to St. Francis Hospital to visit a friend, I noticed a man standing outside near a tree, unzipping his pants to urinate. He looked up at me and said, "I'm so embarrassed. I'm so sorry. I just don't know where else to go."

Under Matrix, he was a criminal.

Frank Jordan's Matrix crackdown concentrated on downtown business areas, and had the goal of moving the homeless out of Union Square, the Civic Center, and other prime locations where his supporters maintained businesses. The result was the end of homeless encampments, the temporary end of the homeless in Union Square, but not the end of homelessness. Instead, the homeless ended up in neighborhoods throughout San Francisco, in other business districts where owners lacked the same clout as Jordan's downtown friends.

When Jordan first ordered the Matrix crackdown, he set up a police barricade, complete with armed officers, around city hall in anticipation of riots by the homeless. I was called home from a state Democratic Party finance meeting in La Costa that day for the "homeless rioting." To get into my office in San Francisco City Hall, I had to walk through a cordon of more than two dozen tactical-squad police units standing in a line atop the building's front steps.

There were no homeless people there. The police were guarding city hall and a jittery Frank Jordan from an uprising that never materialized. Perhaps the homeless were too busy trying to stay alive and hang on to some shred of sanity to show up. Perhaps they were already heading for Golden Gate Park and the city's less touristy shopping districts to escape the police. But Jordan wasn't taking any chances.

I saw Jordan walking upstairs to his office and asked him, "What the hell did I just go through downstairs? What's that army doing in front of city hall?"

Jordan answered, "Well, we've started the Matrix crackdown and we're afraid some people might not like it."

"What Matrix crackdown?"

Jordan told me that he was arresting people for the four quality-of-life crimes. I was stunned. I thought he must be kidding. But he wasn't.

The mayor's paranoia over some kind of attack by homeless people shows the damage that can be caused by manufacturing imaginary criminals where none had existed before. If a person, or an entire class of people, is continuously treated like a criminal, is referred to by our leaders with contempt in the media, and is the target of programs under which he or she is arrested—and who gets arrested besides criminals?—then that person becomes a criminal in the eyes of citizens and, especially, police. Matrix in particular was zealously enforced by many officers of the San Francisco Police Department. One cop, part of a group keeping an eye on a food wagon set up in protest at city hall by the relief group Food Not Bombs, took it upon himself to kick a cup of soup from the hand of 83-year-old Cynthia Mays, a woman who was clearly not a criminal.

I was furious that he had no understanding at all about how this woman might be humiliated by this. I said, "Did you go to the academy for this? Did you go to cop school so you could kick old ladies? What the hell's wrong with you? What if she was your mother?" This last question really got him. "I hope to hell your mother doesn't end up in the street with a cup of soup in her hand and have some bully walk up and kick it away."

The next day, Cynthia was waiting for me outside city hall. She told me the police had come back and taken away and crushed her only real possession, a framed photograph of her son. Department of Public Works trucks, operating under Matrix, were being used to cart away and destroy the possessions of homeless people who had been cited.

Connie Chung did a CBS report on my confrontation with the police officer. It portrayed the mayor's program as inhumane, and the police as fanatics. The taste of Matrix inevitably began to sour for some of its supporters—though not all of them.

After this confrontation, I began work on legislation condemning and rescinding Matrix. I would later receive the support of only two of my fellow supervisors, Terence Hallinan and Sue Bierman. Jordan had convinced the other eight supervisors that the business interests who were at the real heart of Matrix were too valuable to the city to alienate. He also wanted to be perceived as being tough on "crime."

I didn't ask the city attorney to approve the legislation. I didn't care what her legal opinion was. I knew she would spout the party line. Instead, I went to every single one of my colleagues and asked for their support.

Doors slammed in my face. Apart from Hallinan and Bierman, all I heard was the "business, business, business" refrain. Bums, I was told, were bad for business; they scared the tourists away from shop fronts. The vote was eight to three against me. So much for San Francisco's reputation for progressive government.

Six months later, after nine *thousand* Matrix citations had been issued—creating a situation in which imaginary criminals were in danger of becoming real criminals by not responding to the citations—I wrote legislation granting amnesty for Matrix violators. I stood before the rest of the board of supervisors and tried to appeal to my colleagues' sense of compassion.

Where are you supposed to urinate if you don't have a home and they don't let you in restaurants because you're homeless? It's not me or you walking into restaurants and asking to use the bathroom. It's a homeless person. What are you supposed to do? Tell your body that you don't have to go? And what are you supposed to do when it's ten o'clock at night and you've knocked on the door asking for shelter from the city and the city says there's no room at the inn? What exactly are you supposed to do? How are you supposed to *not* sleep from ten at night until six in the morning? How are you supposed to keep awake? So you fall asleep, and it's January, and it's freezing, and there's a cardboard box, and you cut it up and put it over your shoulders, and you get in a doorway so the wind doesn't kill you, like it does to the 150 homeless people who die in this city every year from exposure to the elements. What do you do when your government says that you don't have a right to shelter? What do you do? Not be human? Not sleep? Not urinate? And what is the government giving these people as alternatives to being homeless?

When it came time to vote, I put my head in my hands in anger and frustration. The vote was five to four. Shortly after that, a Tom Meyer cartoon in the *San Francisco Chronicle* showed Saint Francis leaving San Francisco via the Golden Gate Bridge, pushing a shopping cart. This loss affected me emotionally more than any other—I couldn't help feeling I'd let the people of the city down.

As a result of my opposition to Matrix, I was condemned as an everything-but-a-commie radical left-winger. Matrix was cleaning up the streets and the downtown merchants loved it.

I could only sit and watch.

Mario Cuomo, one of the few politicians I respect, once said that, while a successful politician might quietly take action to help the poor, he must publicly ignore them. They're politically ruinous. As

I read the newspapers in frustration, following the reports of Matrix violators being rounded up, I almost believed it.

Of course, neither Matrix nor the dozens of similar programs throughout the country do anything to eliminate homelessness. Their real effect is simply to drive homeless people to other neighborhoods during crackdowns. And once Matrix and its cousins have driven the homeless away from targeted areas and enforcement is relaxed, the homeless move back and the cycle begins again.

There are more intelligent and effective ways to deal with homelessness. If we find out who composes the ranks of the homeless, study the causes of homelessness, and then use this information to shape policies and programs, government can effectively attack the problem on several fronts.

Mother Teresa was once asked how she took care of so many thousands of poor people. Her response, "One by one," inspired my own plan to combat homelessness, designed as a compassionate and sensible alternative to Matrix. With the help of my staff, especially Reg Smith, and numerous community groups, and drawing on more than two years of research, I developed an outline for a coordinated plan to house 3,000 additional people in the city. This included veterans, women and children, people with medical and mental health conditions, seniors, and the undereducated and underemployed. In addition, it called for long-term, permanent solutions as well as strategies for preventing new homelessness.

My plan proposed active outreach and engagement, short-term emergency housing centers, and the transfer of all city facilities operations to community-based housing and care providers for transitional and permanent housing. Education and prevention were important features of One by One. And because until then the city had lacked a formal plan to deal with homelessness and had relied instead on a police crackdown, we'd been unable to receive significant funds from Washington, so a key facet of the plan was to form cooperative partnerships with community organizations to aggressively seek federal resources.

In addition, housing and employment components were to be developed through legislation to provide quick permits for providers, rent ordinance/zoning amendments for shared housing, community housing, and employee on-site training. The plan also called for the establishment of separate housing components for people with TB, AIDS, and substance abuse and mental health problems, and a resolution asking churches, synagogues, and mosques to join in a partnership to provide additional beds.

All the funding necessary to implement the plan would come from the federal government, churches, businesses, charitable organizations, and money already allocated by the city to provide shelter. San Francisco was already spending $49 million a year for shelter facilities, but hadn't put a dent in the homelessness problem. I demonstrated that for the amount of money already being spent on shelters, the San Francisco Holiday Inn could accommodate the same number of people with maid and room service for a year. Obviously, money has been pouring through the cracks, and with it, an unconscionable number of people.

Cleaning up the problem of homelessness involves more than simply finding a place for people to stay. Under Walden House, Hamilton Family Center, and Progress Foundation, three progressive San Francisco programs, people are given a place to live and get back on their feet for two or three months, then helped to find work. The mission of these organizations is to get people out of the shelter and into temporary housing, which makes the process of getting back into the job market far more manageable. They have a phenomenal success rate, and would be an integral part of One by One.

We should never allow solutions to become traps for the homeless. To guard against this, One by One calls for linking the priority eligibility for city supplements and rental assistance to training in health care and graduation from homeless employment programs. The plan prescribed a two-pronged approach: putting training and assistance programs in place, and ensuring that low-cost housing would be permanently and readily available for those who made the transition.

Will this plan eradicate all homelessness? There will always be a small minority of homeless people who are young and able-bodied and who refuse help getting off the streets, who say they make more money begging than they could at a job, or who are too hardened by crime and drugs and their misery to be helped. Yet in their fervor to "eradicate" homelessness, local governments must not take an unenlightened approach to the problem by assuming that the mentally ill, the mother forced out of her house, and the man trapped by addiction are all on the street through their own fault or choice.

Few examples better illustrate the dangers of criminalizing the poor than the story of Father Alfred Boeddeker, the founder of St. Anthony's Dining Room in the crime-ridden Tenderloin neighborhood of San Francisco. I feel a special affinity with Father Boeddeker, because St. Anthony was from Padua—my husband's birthplace. One day many years ago, as Father Boeddeker knelt in prayer before the statue of St. Anthony, he distinctly heard the statue say "Feed me." In his writings Father Boeddeker said that he realized that St. Anthony had meant "Feed the people." So in 1950 he established St. Anthony's Dining Room.

Father Boeddeker's passing at age 90 came during my fight with Frank Jordan over Matrix. His funeral at St. Boniface Church was attended by many important Californians. San Francisco Archbishop John Quinn sat in the sanctuary. I sat with my son Joe next to Jordan in the front pew. The back of the church was packed with homeless people—the same people that Father Boeddeker had fed and sheltered. We were all there to honor a great man who had devoted his life to caring for the poor.

Yet the politicians and dignitaries in attendance that afternoon had, throughout their careers, mostly been silent in speaking of the need to do something—anything—substantial to improve the lives of homeless people. And as speaker after speaker extolled Father Boeddeker's achievements and decried our leaders' lack of compassion for the poor, every one of those politicians and community leaders acted as if they'd been kicked in the stomach. Quinn, who had been responsible for closing churches and canceling programs across the city, looked as though he wanted to disappear.

A young Franciscan monk who spoke at the service invoked Jesus by quoting from the New Testament: "When I was hungry, you fed me. When I was homeless, you gave me shelter." Seeing all these officials listen to the words, and knowing the reality of the homeless in San Francisco and all over the country, I was struck by the irony of the situation. Men and women and children were sleeping on doorsteps because of policy, and these politicians, feeling the shame of their hypocrisy, were paying hollow lip service to a man who would have hated what they did to the homeless.

A few days after the funeral, another Tom Meyer cartoon appeared in the *San Francisco Chronicle*, depicting some homeless people at Holy Cross Cemetery planting a flower on Father Boeddeker's grave. Behind them, police are rushing forward to arrest them.

COURTESY OF TOM MEYER

Eventually, city businesses started turning against Matrix. It became unpopular as it grew more and more apparent among the city's voters that the crackdown was little more than political smoke and mirrors, and that something more lasting and compassionate had to be done.

Frank Jordan lost the 1995 mayoral election in San Francisco largely because of his stance on homelessness. Willie Brown had endorsed One by One during his campaign, but soon after taking office he abandoned the plan, calling the homeless problem "unsolvable," despite the fact that I offered whatever help he needed in implementing One by One.

It ought to be obvious to everyone by now that as real wages continue to fall, corporate downsizing (read: firings) has become *de rigueur*, the disastrous welfare reform law has been signed by Clinton, and the misdirected wars on drugs and crime—with their emphasis on punishment rather than education—look increasingly like losing battles, the homeless population is going to increase. We must take the next step and begin to treat homeless people with the compassion and understanding that is the due of any human being.

Homeless people are by no means the only manufactured criminals in America. In our search for someone to blame for our general and unfocused feelings of unease, we have allowed our leaders to pillory any and every group that is politically weaker than the middle class. Over the past few years, real wages have fallen, and the end of the Cold War has left us without a traditional, identifiable enemy. Groups like welfare recipients, youth, minorities, aliens both legal and undocumented, the mentally ill, gays, and even poets and artists now somehow symbolize a danger to the American family. Clearly, any individual who threatens someone else, who waves a gun in anger or would try to lure a child into a car with a piece of candy, is a criminal, and ought to be treated as one. There are plenty of real threats to our safety and economic well-being without having to make them up out of thin air. Yet when you brand a gay man, for instance, or a young person, or an immigrant a "danger," then you are labeling an entire group of people. That's the real crime.

In the fiscally austere 1990s, politicians on both sides of the aisle have managed to turn an entire class of people—politically powerless people—into criminals in the public's mind. Without offering up any factual numbers, Republicans have cast welfare recipients in the role of villain in their efforts to oversimplify the country's financial turmoil, and Democrats have been complicit in pandering to this politically powerful strategy. The real villains, of course, are not a group of poor people who are allotted a meager 1% of our federal budget for food and shelter for themselves and their children. But corporations, who pay the re-election bills of our leaders, prefer easily defined enemies; then the harsh spotlight of public anger turns away from themselves—and those leaders. It is now, as it has always been, easier and safer to blame the helpless for our woes. The welfare "reform" bill of 1996 is an example of misdirection; to his credit, though, President Clinton felt as though he had to apologize for signing it, and will likely take steps to reduce its sting. Nevertheless, most experts agree that the ranks of the homeless are going to swell because of the new law. Children are going to be particularly hard hit.

In accepting the manufactured criminality of the poor, we have allowed politicians to dehumanize these people, to turn them into, at best, lazy and irresponsible do-nothings and, at worst, monsters. Twenty years ago, Republican politicians continually repeated the mantra of "Cadillac-driving welfare mothers" in an attempt to demonize those who received federal assistance. Today AFDC mothers are typically portrayed as baby factories who keep producing children so that they can file for increased cash benefits. Research has shown, though, that poor women have a lot of children simply because they are poorer and more poorly educated, not as a means of additional income. This is apparent in states that do not increase benefits with each additional child.

107

Our specific images of people on welfare are fueled partly by politicians, partly by the media, and partly by our own biases and misconceptions. A recent poll shows that the average American believes that over 50% of the federal budget goes to welfare, when in fact it is less than 1%. Most Americans also believe that the majority of welfare recipients are African American. Face it: when we read about a person on welfare in the paper, we automatically assume the person is African American. Of course, the fact is that only a quarter of welfare recipients are African American. Half are white.

Some politicians would have us believe that welfare recipients are, naturally, lazy people who would much rather accept a handout and walk down to the market and buy a bottle of booze than get out and look for a job. It is easier to cut benefits to poor people if we think these people are poor through their own fault. California Governor Pete Wilson has acted particularly heartlessly, dismissing the impact of his cuts in welfare over the years by saying, "Let them drink one less beer!" Yet 50% of people who receive welfare are either children or over the age of 65. And surveys among poor people consistently show that an overwhelming majority who *can* work are desperate for a job—welfare recipients recognize the fact that they are trapped in a cycle of poverty, and are as critical of other welfare recipients as the middle class is.

The need for welfare reform is obvious. As long as people are better off under welfare than they are with a full-time minimum-wage job, and as long as corporate America demands a constant 6% unemployment rate to ensure the health of Wall Street, then people will abuse the system. For those men and women not saddled with children or poor health, restrictions like a time limit on benefits might be helpful. But we need to couple such changes with other government guarantees, such as job training and child care services. And we must remember that poor women with children who feel pain and hunger and loneliness and scorn. Their children suffer malnutrition and are at grave risk of being lost to violence and drugs. These people—these women, the poorest and weakest group in America—are most in need of our help and compassion.

The values of America do not include kicking people when they are down.

Like the poor, teens and children are often used by politicians as a convenient focus for blame and fear. Children, with no legal political voice (they can't vote) are an easy target. Politicians consistently portray young people as either actual or potential criminals, and now, when crime among young adults is actually declining, our leaders have seized upon youth crime as a pressing issue. While crime committed by minors is a real problem, it should not be twisted into an occasion for scapegoating.

The public's tolerance of youth crime has been eroded over the last five years or so by politicians looking for social Band-Aids and by a press that is eager for sensational stories. Two eight-year-old boys toss their six-year-old playmate out a window, and a few more states enact laws to lower the minimum age at which a child can be tried as an adult. The age for which a child can be tried for murder is now as low as eight in some states, and one or two states have stripped their statutes of any minimum age at all.

Yet is a six-year-old Richmond, California, boy capable of understanding the charge of attempted murder against him for beating nearly to death a newborn infant? And is he actually guilty of an act that requires premeditation and knowledge of right and wrong?

As a society, we have always feared our youth. They are unpredictable, after all, and prone to unacceptable behavior as a result of influence by peers, the media, and violent parents. In the 1950s, gangs of hooligans on motorcycles were a great suburban fear; in the 1960s it was drug-crazed hippies. Today the object of our terror wears an African American or Latino face and carries a gun and is willing to shoot anybody for looking at them the wrong way. We take our own children out of public schools because of this image, justified or not. We avoid walking in certain poor neighborhoods at night, or even during daylight. We call for censorship of certain rap and rock albums.

Though in some respects caution is called for—I wouldn't go walking around the Geneva Towers neighborhood of San Francisco at night, for example; dangers do exist that we must be aware of— the degree to which our fear of youth has been inflamed is preposterous. Every child on the bus is not packing heat; every group of children standing outside McDonald's is not looking to make a crack sale. Children are children. As citizens, we must demand that youth be treated as responsible people, that politicians look on them as constituents to whom they are beholden. At this key point in their lives, they stand a good chance of becoming responsible adults and productive members of the community—if they are treated with fairness and respect.

I have always believed this—I have four children of my own, after all, and I have seen how children turn into good grown-ups, despite the pressures and pitfalls of childhood. I have authored a number of pieces of youth legislation in San Francisco and created the children's budget, despite both active and passive resistance from two successive mayors, Art Agnos and Frank Jordan, and a number of my fellow supervisors.

I think these people just don't want to try to understand children—or maybe children are just too tempting a scapegoat.

When my plan for the children's budget met opposition from Agnos, I took it to the people of San Francisco directly as city Proposition J and it passed, demonstrating that people are tired of living with the kind of fear and misunderstanding that our leaders and the media constantly try to sell us. Proposition J's passing meant, among other things, a hot meal a day for homeless children and bus fare for disabled youth. It's harder to see young people as criminals when they're humanized, as this legislation proves.

In 1995, I pressed for the creation of a youth commission, which would create a body of children responsible for reviewing proposed legislation that directly involved San Francisco's youth, including curfew and truancy laws. Reg Smith, my legislative aide, pushed unwaveringly for this legislation. In the face of the assertions of Supervisor Sue Bierman that children weren't responsible enough to execute the duties of a city commission, and the tacit agreement of the majority of the board that she was right, I took this proposition to the ballot in 1995. It passed with 71% of the vote.

The new commissioners came to my office the following summer and requested a $150,000 budget. The document that that able and confident group of young people presented to me—and it included details of salary and meeting location expenses—was one of the cleanest budgets I've ever seen.

It was overwhelmingly approved.

The resistance I have met from other politicians in passing pro-child legislation reflects a general attitude of mistrust toward youth, who must prove themselves after they have already been judged. Instead of being seen as both current and future resources in our communities, youth face an exhausting uphill battle for acceptance. They're labeled in negative ways by public officials who never even try to connect to youth culture and, in failing to respect their needs, create the potential for real criminals down the line.

Poorly planned curfew laws illustrate this fact. In setting a time after which children are arrested for being on the street without making sure that children have a place to be at night, we are neglecting to fulfill what should be the rationale behind curfews in the first place. It is not enough that children are simply out of sight at 11 o'clock, or whenever. If a child has no real home to speak of, where is he supposed to be? If his parents are violent drunks, why should he happily trot home when the sun goes down? As they now stand, our fear-inspired laws turn a child into a criminal—with a record—simply for being out of doors after dark. We must prevent the criminalizing of these children by getting them off the streets and putting them somewhere safe.

So much for the Republican-inspired ridicule of "wasteful" projects like midnight basketball.

Criminalizing children puts them in danger of violence themselves, both immediately and in the future. Like homeless people, children can become a target for overzealous law enforcement. And once you put a child in handcuffs, you've created a history, a potential for real anger, and a distrust of authority. Curfew laws accomplish just that.

Henry, an African American high school student, was part of a group that was arrested at Fisherman's Wharf in San Francisco at 11:15 on the night of their high school prom a couple of years ago. Henry's friends were all released to their parents, but Henry's folks were out of town. He was jailed from Saturday night until Tuesday. During those 60 hours that 16-year-old child was repeatedly raped.

I can't count how many ways that authorities dropped the ball on that one, from the cops who put Henry in a cell with real criminals to the lawmakers who passed a bad law in the first place, proving they can't think things through beyond the latest opinion poll.

It's easy to ascribe criminal behavior to an entire group such as young people. The media always goes for the sensational story; we are terrified of crime to such an extent that we welcome an identifiable group to avoid, and children have no political voice. Never mind that the odds of the average person being attacked by a child with a gun are statistically nonexistent. Just get them all off the streets after a certain hour—out of sight, out of mind.

Don't we all feel safer now?

All the energy political leaders have wasted in creating imaginary crime and criminals has come at the expense of fighting real crime.

When police are ordered to spend their time harassing homeless people or rounding up young people for wearing pagers, they're not out on the streets stopping domestic violence and investigating murders.

Never let it be said that I think we ought to coddle criminals. I generally support legislation like California's "three strikes" law, although the law should be amended to reflect mandatory sentencing for three *violent* felonies only. No one should be sent to Pelican Bay for the rest of his life for stealing a bicycle from the Stanford University campus—something that actually happened. I also agree with the recent decision handed down by the California Supreme Court stipulating that the law gives prosecutors more power than judges in determining sentencing.

As a citizen and a crime victim—I've been stalked on a number of occasions—I want to see an increase in the real prevention of crime and, when prevention fails, criminals behind bars. Richard Allen Davis should never have been allowed out of prison to kidnap and murder Polly Klaas. When a killer's own lawyers argue before a jury that their client should never have been released from prison, you know that something's wrong with the system.

Punishment is a necessary component of our criminal justice system, of course. But too much emphasis is placed on punishment at the expense of prevention. When Clinton's crime bill was passed by Congress in 1994, the issue of prevention came to light—and was roundly derided by Republicans. The conservative Congress of 1995 voted to kill almost the entire law, including a nonpartisan provision that would have allocated money to put 100,000 additional cops on the streets of our cities. Study after study has shown that simply having more cops around lowers crime—that's why I have pushed for maximum police staffing—yet prevention as basic as this is seen as being soft on crime.

It's politically expedient to cram the prisons full of people until they are illegally overcrowded, then spend billions of taxpayer dollars to build more.

Do harsher sentences deter crime? Most studies have shown they do not—and that includes the death penalty. Texas, which executes more criminals than all the other states combined, still has the highest murder rate in the country. And "three strikes" in California has not appreciably reduced the violent crime rate. But prevention programs have consistently produced results in the form of a much lower rate of crime among participants.

Why are people like Richard Allen Davis released from prison? One reason is prison overcrowding and accompanying mandatory release orders. The Constitution forbids cruel and unusual treatment of prisoners, and four people living in a cell designed to hold one person should be considered cruel and unusual by any rational human being.

And who is it that is packing our prisons in uncountable numbers? Murderers? Rapists? Kidnappers? The vast majority of prisoners in U.S. jails are drug offenders, sentenced under mandatory minimum sentencing, even for such minor infractions as simple possession. States like Michigan have enacted "zero-tolerance" laws that stipulate life in prison with no chance for parole for selling a minimal amount of drugs. No such law exists for any other first felony in America. So when it's time to kick out more hardened prisoners to make room for the new guys, who gets let out? Richard Allen Davis, a convicted sex offender eligible for parole—not the college kid who sold his buddies a little pot.

This is not to suggest that drugs are just fine, or that drug-related crimes are in some way victimless. Millions of children take drugs, and they are victims in anybody's book. There is an enormous amount of lost potential there, even among children who use only occasionally. But if we are going to get serious about reducing drug use, throwing everybody in prison is not going to work. It's an impossibility. And the simple fact of the matter is that *millions* would end up in prison if rabid war-on-drugs politicians had their way. If you doubt me, just stroll down Haight Street some warm Friday evening, or stand on a corner in the Mission, or attend a posh gala in a Pacific Heights mansion.

By this time it's a lib-dem cliché to call for studying the legalization of drugs, although some conservative pundits like George Will have begun to advocate the idea. But if you put two criminals side by side, one who was busted for possession of dope and one who raped a teenager, you would probably have little trouble choosing which one you'd want back out on the street.

Yet drug offenders are sentenced, on average, to longer prison terms than sex offenders. Obviously, the answer is more than simply a matter of giving people carte blanche to stuff handfuls of drugs into their bodies; we need to choose, as a society, who is going to receive the full attention of the criminal justice system, and who would benefit more from preventive programs. Drug abuse prevention and treatment are always more effective than prison. If you decriminalize and regulate drugs, then an entire class of actual criminals—drug dealers—are eliminated. And once they are eliminated, drug-related violence disappears.

Once the money we now use in rounding up the usual suspects is diverted to treatment and prevention programs like Walden House, drug use patterns will mirror what we've seen in smoking patterns: education works at keeping people from starting the habit, and detox programs are increasingly more effective in getting people to stop. We need only look as far as the Netherlands, which has decriminalized drug possession and which has a phenomenal record of treatment and prevention.

Does anyone believe the war on drugs has done anything to curtail drug use? Any gains we've made in curbing the sale and use of hard drugs have come through prevention, specifically education. Throwing a person in jail for dealing is not going to keep children from using drugs, and anyone who thinks otherwise is deluding himself. Those users are simply going to find another source. And the people at the top of the cycle, the real criminals, are going to make sure another source is available. The war on drugs has barely touched the real power—drug use surveys released in 1996 prove that. Our own government has supported the men and governments of other countries—Manuel Noriega springs to mind as one example—involved in the drug trade. I'm not sure our leaders even believe in the war on drugs any more, if they ever did.

They just want to be seen as tough on crime.

In November 1994 a survivalist gun nut decided to steal a car and drive to the wealthy San Francisco neighborhood of Pacific Heights with his collection of automatic weapons to kill as many rich people as he could. He got only one: working-class cop James Guelff, who didn't make enough money to afford a Pacific Heights house. He was shot while trying desperately to reload his revolver.

The convoluted process by which we legislate crime is nowhere better illustrated than in the fight to prevent what is indisputably the most terrifying crime of all: the random act of murder. The Long Island Railway, 101 California, the Stockton schoolyard—these are the ones that make the front pages. These are the crimes that we fear most.

There is only one way to stop crimes like these. Prevention isn't going to catch mad killers early. The threat of long prison sentences or even death won't make them think twice.

These people must never be allowed to possess a gun.

I'm not talking about some cosmetic ban on a couple dozen types of machine guns. I'm talking about laws that keep all guns from being indiscriminately sold to anyone. Yes, we now have the Brady

Law and a waiting period. But that is strictly for retail sale at a gun shop. Anyone who passes a background check can buy any number of guns, then take those guns to a gun show and sell them to anyone who has the cash.

Do people think that the Long Island Railway killer bothered going through legal channels?

The National Rifle Association (NRA) is correct in one thing: the Brady Bill is not terribly efficient at keeping guns out of the hands of those determined to get them. Children in my city can buy a gun from a friend for practically nothing, or they can borrow or rent one from local gangs. And my city is considered relatively safe.

But the NRA's solution is to increase penalties for committing crimes with a gun. I'm sure the thought of something worse than California's death penalty would have stopped the Pacific Heights shooter.

Right.

The NRA and their apologists are living in a fantasy world.

We must have stringent gun laws. It's that simple. A gun license ought to be the most difficult license to earn, harder to get than a driver's license or a pilot's license, certainly more difficult than simply proving you're not a convicted felon. If a person wants to benefit from the Second Amendment, he ought to be willing and able to show himself to be a responsible citizen. Beyond that, he should *by law* be prohibited from buying some ridiculous piece of semiautomatic murderous weaponry; a simple handgun or rifle or shotgun is clearly sufficient for meeting the NRA's stated goal of preserving target and sport shooting and home defense. He ought to be forced *by law* to keep his gun under lock and key to prevent it from being accidentally fired by a child into a playmate's head. He should be required *by law* to register his gun with authorities and to know of its whereabouts at all times. And he ought to be forbidden *by law* to resell it indiscriminately. Anyone breaking these laws ought to face stiff penalties.

117

Yet these rational changes to the law are as remote as a walk on Mars.

When Congress takes decades, kicking and screaming all the way, to finally pass a law as innocuous and commonsensical as the Brady Bill, something is wrong. The truth is simple, of course, when you get down to it: money. Politicians on both sides have traditionally accepted money from the NRA, one of the most powerful lobbies in America, and the NRA represents gun manufacturers' interests— and their interests are considerable.

There are 200 million guns in this country.

No, real change is not likely, because while politicians are talking about the urgent need to fight crime, they are refusing to enact laws that would disarm criminals. When I passed legislation ensuring that all San Francisco cops would be armed with semiautomatic pistols instead of the type of gun that Officer James Guelff was trying to reload when he was murdered, many of my fellow politicians thought the law was a bad idea because of the cost involved. Of course, those politicians backed by the NRA are going to oppose legislation such as this, because if you have a capable, well-armed police force, you may not feel the same burning need to go out and buy three or four Uzis to protect your family—and gun manufacturers' profits would decline accordingly.

So who's really coddling criminals here?

In our attempts to put a face on our anxieties, we have allowed our leaders to demonize the politically powerless, those who are different and, especially, those with less financial clout. I could devote another 50 pages to some of the other groups, including the mentally ill, ethnic minorities (for whom the situation is marginally improving, at least officially), gay men and lesbians (who, in starting to test the reach of their newfound political voices, are being subjected to the worst organized backlash since forced racial segregation in the 1930s and 1940s), immigrants, medicinal marijuana users, and artists like Robert Mapplethorpe and their defenders. Conservative politicians roar that these groups are somehow responsible for all the ills that plague America. Think about it: How many mainstream politicians accuse multinational companies of being at the root of the problem? Or intolerant religious groups? Or a defense budget larger than our five most likely enemies' budgets *combined?* Even when a "radical" right-wing politician occasionally gets it right about things like corporate America, he aligns himself with groups like the Christian Coalition and the NRA.

We must never allow people who have committed no crime to be stamped as criminals simply because they are weaker than we are. This country is great specifically because of its capacity for tolerance and mercy towards those who are different and traditionally misunderstood. We can't forget that the first European Americans were people much like those we now criminalize—people who were made unwelcome in their own homeland, who came here to found a country based not on people's similarities, but on their diversity.

We have allowed the war against real crime to become intolerably politicized. Our leaders have taken a grassroots issue and turned it into a re-election tool. In truth, violent crime rates are dropping, and have been doing so for years. Good news doesn't sell newspapers, though, and horrific sensationalized cases like Polly Klaas's murder whip up public fear and rage. Some responses to public outcry are warranted: I introduced the legislation that created the Child Abduction Unit in the San Francisco District Attorney's Office, which has reunited nearly 150 abducted children with their families. Even if crime rates are declining, one kidnapped child is too many. Yet in the politicized circus of the criminal justice system, Mayor Frank Jordan defunded the program. Assemblyman John Burton fought a bill, which I supported, that extended the penalty for kidnapping.

The public knows little about the realities of crime, and it's not in politicians' best interests to tell them the truth: that crime, though a real problem, is essential to politicians as an issue. Why else do our leaders bat the issue back and forth, ignoring obvious solutions, and spin crime out of thin air where no crime actually exists?

What is it about crime and politics that prevents our thinking clearly, our taking the shortest direct route to eliminating crime from our streets?

Politicians are smart enough to know that the days of campaigning on the platform that everything is going pretty well are long gone. Crime sells, and politicians are elected on law-and-order platforms. In Texas, the current governor was elected partly because he vowed to pull the electric-chair switch more frequently than his opponent. Politicians and candidates need a constant source of crime to point a finger at, and it's expedient to point that finger at noncriminals a lot of the time, or ignore the real causes and solutions of actual crimes.

Crime is a problem that needs addressing. But the real solutions are not at the back end, after the crime has been committed. I discovered soon after I came to politics that if money is a limited resource, then it makes good sense to spend a dollar to prevent a problem instead of spending a thousand dollars to fix it.

If the real goal of "tough on crime" politicians was to eliminate crime, crime might not be the object of fear that it is. We would be spending far more money on schools than on prisons, our courts wouldn't be so clogged, and people would not be so terrified of guns that they feel the need to go out and buy ten of them.

The solutions we need demand fundamental changes in our system, changes that address the economic and educational roots of the problems of crime, both real and imaginary. And if this is a scary prospect, then we should also be examining the alternative.

What will my city look like in 20 years? What about our towns and villages? What direction are we going to take from here? Because we are reaching a point of overload, when either actual crime or the fear of it is going to turn this country into a nation of fear and prisons and weapons and police and, ultimately, walls between *us* and *them*. We've already started down this path.

What will it take for us to turn back?

THE ABYSS:
HEALTH CARE AND AIDS

Through that gross and murky air I spied
A shape come swimming up, that might have quell'd
The stoutest heart with wonder.

INFERNO, CANTO XVI

IN THE *INFERNO*, a deep chasm separates the souls of the violent from those of the fraudulent. That chasm—the Abyss—is a terrifying place, perhaps the most terrifying in the poem, because what lies in it is so far away and so obscure that it can't be made out.

It is this place into which I put what is likely the toughest problem we face as a nation—our health. America's health care costs are the highest in the world. Our health industry is bloated beyond recognition. A sixth of all Americans are uninsured. And, though great strides are being made to cure and prevent disease, we are still ravaged by AIDS, heart disease, cancer, and tobacco-related illnesses. As our population ages and people live longer and longer lives, these problems will only become more serious. We must examine and change our current system. It is flawed beyond belief. It simply denies treatment to those who can't afford it, helping enlarge the rift between the haves and have-nots in this country. Finally, it is so large and so complex that most Americans don't even want to try to figure it out.

But we must understand what lies at the bottom of the Abyss if we are safely to cross it.

The art of politics would seem to demand that officeholders be willing to take a hard look at current and future needs and make the difficult choices that best serve the people, even in a world of competing interests. Most politicians, however, ignore approaching problems and lack the vision or the will to attempt substantive changes. When they do take the initiative, it's usually only because the public or powerful lobbying groups have pushed them into it.

Under these circumstances, the balance of power shifts and change becomes inevitable. This is what's been happening in the case of tobacco; the opposition to the industry has become too strong to ignore. As a result, on this particular issue, many politicians are beginning to act for the common good.

This rarely occurs, though. For some issues, competing interests are so strong that they create political gridlock. This is what's happened with health care.

Proponents of our current health care system claim that America has the most advanced medical care in the world. They say that we have the finest doctors, hospitals, and technology, that our physicians routinely perform the most complex transplants and other surgical procedures, and that we are more successful than any other nation in treating cancer and other serious illnesses. They also point out that most Americans can get health care in some form, through their employer, individual coverage, or—in the case of the poor or elderly—Medicaid and Medicare. Therefore, they argue, there is no problem.

They're wrong. Although most of us do receive adequate—and, in some cases, even excellent—medical services, there are grave problems in the system that are not being addressed. The current trends suggest that we're heading toward disaster. First, there is the problem of the uninsured: millions of Americans lack medical insurance. Second is the issue of maintaining quality of care in the face of skyrocketing costs, the fiscal crisis of Medicare, and corporate greed and profiteering in the health care industry. Third is the continued political posturing that has blocked intelligent, compassionate responses to the needs of those with life-threatening illnesses such as AIDS and cancer. Underlying these trends is the unfounded belief on the part of many political leaders and much of the public that certain groups of people in this country bring on their own health problems, that it's up to those people to pay the costs, and that they're somehow disposable and should be forgotten.

These issues are interrelated, and underneath them all is a combination of self-interest, greed, and the inability or unwillingness of our political leaders to seek out reasonable solutions. This combination is widening the Abyss every day, and it will take a bridge of honest, clear-eyed dialogue to cross it.

One of the problems that's been avoided for too long is the lack of universal access to health care. This is a problem not just for the more than 40 million Americans who are uninsured but for all of us, because we are all affected financially in one way or another.

Who are the uninsured? Some are the unemployed, who may be too poor to afford private insurance but not poor enough to qualify for government-paid coverage. Most of the uninsured, however, are workers in the one-quarter of businesses in this country that do not provide medical coverage for their employees. A recent study found that about 70% of the uninsured had been employed for at least some of the time that they were without health insurance. These are the people who may not qualify for employee-paid health benefits and who may not make enough to pay for food, housing, and health insurance on their own. Many of those surveyed had worked for employers who provided coverage to at least some employees. According to the American Hospital Association the number of uninsured Americans has increased in recent years because many employers have cut back or eliminated coverage to full-time employees or have hired more part-time workers without health benefits. In addition, according to the Economic and Social Research Institute in Washington, there is a trend toward reducing or eliminating coverage for the families of employees, even among those businesses that continue to provide health insurance for employees.

Some people think this isn't a problem because they assume that the uninsured can get free medical care for serious illness or injury. That's a fallacy. Some 53% of uninsured adults reported problems getting or paying for their health care in 1995, and 45% of the uninsured needed care and could not get it. And these aren't people with minor problems; it's the sickest people who are most likely to have problems getting the medical care they desperately need.

Not surprisingly, the uninsured can rarely afford preventive health care, regular checkups, or treatment for minor illnesses. As a result, many are stricken with minor illnesses that become major illnesses, which then must be treated in hospital emergency rooms. Hospitals either turn such patients away outright or temporarily absorb the costs of treatment before passing the costs on to other patients in the form of higher hidden fees.

In many instances, untreated illnesses lead to temporary or even permanent loss of employment for those who become sick. Eventually, some of these uninsured and their families cross the boundary into poverty and into government assistance programs. And those attempting to get off welfare by taking low-paid jobs that lack health benefits may soon find themselves thrust back into poverty with the family's first serious medical problem.

Even those of us who are insured have no guarantee that our health care costs will be completely covered. In the face of catastrophic illness, many individuals and families with group coverage find that they are paying higher and higher co-payments or that fewer conditions are being covered. People with individual coverage may also find themselves inadequately covered or soon discover either that they are now "uninsurable" or that their continued coverage comes with steep increases that they can't afford. The quality of coverage may diminish as a person switches jobs, has a change in health, or simply ages. No one is safe.

Many people in this country who appear to be doing okay financially are really just one paycheck from eviction or foreclosure and repossession of their property—one paycheck, therefore, from poverty. And some devastating illnesses, like cancer and AIDS, can instantly devour any savings they have, as well as their ability to make money and to continue paying premiums even if they have insurance. I've met many AIDS patients over the years who were in this position and quickly went from being homeowners to losing everything, all because they were uninsured or underinsured or because they lacked disability insurance or premium payment provisions in their policies. And I've heard from many families in which a medical checkup was postponed, an early diagnosis for a treatable illness not made, because of financial pressures and lack of health insurance.

Some health care activists have called for mandatory employer-paid insurance, but small businesses across the country threaten that closure and layoffs would result. In any event, who would pay coverage for the unemployed? Others have suggested a national health program, similar to Canada's, which guarantees a certain minimum coverage for everyone. But critics scream about "socialized medicine," long waits to see doctors, and reduced quality of care.

No one should have to die because of financial pressures, but this is exactly what's happening as a result of both the gridlock in Washington over health care reform and industry greed. Every special interest group wants protection or a guaranteed piece of the action. The entire industry is in conflict, from doctors to hospitals to pharmaceutical manufacturers to managed-care and health maintenance organizations (HMOs). Every group has its own concerns: small businesses fear that the cost of health reform will come out of their pockets and that they'll be forced to shut down or lay off employees because of higher operating costs; those who are currently insured worry about increased premiums; the health care industry talks about the inefficiencies that would result from further government controls or involvement in health delivery. And all these special interests continue to make their case to congresspeople who, of course, frighten voters in their districts with terms like "socialized medicine" or "tax increase." Consequently, through their inaction, most politicians are casting their vote in favor of a growing abyss of health care. Meanwhile, the status quo continues, and large numbers of people continue to go uninsured or underinsured, some of them receiving a lower quality of care and some of them dying.

Another central health care issue is cost control. Even with some 40 million uninsured Americans, the current cost of health care in this nation is so huge that it's equivalent to the eighth largest economy in the world—larger than the entire economy of Great Britain. For the past several years, health care costs have escalated at a precipitous rate, to the point where we are now spending about 14% of our gross domestic product on health care. This is the highest rate in the world. Britain's is only 6% and Canada's is only 8%. No other industrialized nation spends more than 10%.

We'll undoubtedly continue to see increases in Medicare. In 1992, Medicare costs for older Americans reached $130 billion, up from $88 billion in 1988. Since then, these costs have continued to climb, because more people are getting older while the overall expense of health care has continued to rise. As the older population in America continues to increase, and more people qualify for Medicare, the costs for this government-funded program will either reach astronomical amounts or have to be controlled through severe cost-cutting measures.

In years to come there will also be fewer caregivers and wage earners to support the elderly. Today there are 3.8 million people over 85 years of age—the fastest-growing segment of the population in the country. And the cost of health care for the elderly, when hospitalized, is an average of three times more per event than it is for those under 65 years of age. With these increases, continued quality care for the elderly may well rupture even the most carefully planned program that our society can devise.

Although Medicare costs will clearly need to be controlled, no one's saying how this will be done or what the effects will be on quality of care. Critics talk of eliminating vital services, requiring higher co-payments, and even rationing health care, while politicians use phrases like "reducing payments to physicians and hospitals." The politicians, however, never say what this will really mean in terms of care for the elderly. This is a political hot potato that no one wants to handle, especially because more elderly also means more elderly voters. So the potential for a major crisis continues to grow.

This is both an economic and a moral crisis. Economically, quality health care needs to be paid for by the elderly themselves or their children. And morally, we may well see a true generation gap, with families in the middle having to choose between helping their parents or helping their children. The retired and the elderly are already devalued in our culture; it looks like this trend will only get worse.

Why is quality health care so expensive? Maybe, as President Clinton suggested when he proposed his Health Security Plan in late 1993, "health care is too uncertain and too expensive, too bureaucratic and too wasteful. It has too much fraud and too much greed." Some opponents of the current system estimate that 30% of health expenditures are wasted on administration, profits, marketing, and defensive medicine. Others claim that much of the administrative cost is actually the result of the hundreds of government regulations.

I have a different viewpoint. I believe that the uncontrolled pursuit of profit within the health care industry is chiefly responsible. Health care is not only the fastest-growing industry in America; it has also become a mover on Wall Street. Health care executives are drawing enormous salaries and stock-based compensation packages because of the huge profits they're bringing in.

Clinton's Health Security Plan had two goals: universal coverage and cost control. Supposedly, these would be achieved by requiring employers to provide care and by creating a system of what were termed "managed-care alliances" to minimize duplication of services and eliminate waste. These alliances were expected to keep costs down through organized competition, pushing hospitals and providers into networks. Competition would drive prices down while government would control quality of care. Consumers would benefit because companies would compete for contracts with consumer groups, and they wouldn't be able to pick only healthy members. Instead, the cost of insuring high-risk individuals would be spread around. Further, accountability would be required from all—physicians, hospitals, pharmaceutical companies and manufacturers, and suppliers of medical supplies and equipment.

Unfortunately, because of competing special interests and lobbyists, the Health Security Plan went nowhere. But something interesting happened in the area of cost control. The idea of managed-care alliances caught on, in the form of HMOs and other managed-care organizations as well as in corporate mergers and the rise of huge, centralized, for-profit hospital systems. In fact, more and more Americans—more than 149 million by 1995—have been pushed into managed care, and chances are good that your local hospital is now part of a corporation with a listing on the stock exchange. Indeed, costs have been controlled and the profits of large hospital systems and managed-care organizations have been enormous, but the cost savings have not necessarily been passed on to consumers. And these savings may well have come at the expense of quality of care.

The largest hospital system in the country is Columbia/HCA. In the eight years since it began, it has acquired nearly 350 hospitals. Some might say that reduces duplication and costs. Maybe, but where are these cost savings going? They aren't lowering patients' bills or helping to pay for charity cases.

A lot of the money is going to shareholders: in the third quarter of 1996, Columbia's net income rose to $311 million, up from $274 million in the same quarter in 1995. And in large part, companies' increased profits are going to pay astronomical salaries and to provide stock portfolios to the top executives who broker these deals. These sweetheart salaries are buried within administrative costs. As of May 1996, Richard Scott, the head of Columbia/HCA, held stocks worth $316.4 million, just under a third of a billion dollars. And Scott's a pauper compared to Leonard Abramson, the head of U.S. Health Care, who held stocks totaling $843.5 million. These two men are not unique. With each hospital or HMO merger, top executives in acquiring corporations are often paid massive bonuses, while those in acquired corporations are given platinum parachutes.

Some of the hospitals that are being purchased by for-profit groups like Columbia/HCA are not-for-profit facilities that have long been considered local assets in the community, supported for years by local donations and volunteer efforts. Why would trustees of a not-for-profit hospital sell their local treasure? There seem to be two reasons. First, they often get squeezed out by neighboring for-profit hospitals that have made special lower-cost deals with various HMOs. And second, the trustees themselves are often bought off, provided millions of dollars to share among themselves.

The quality of care provided to the overall community by these corporate hospitals is often questionable. Columbia/HCA has cut staffing levels, bought and then closed hospitals in regions where they owned other facilities, and cut charity care by up to one-third. Nor has this happened only with large hospital groups like Columbia/HCA. In nearly every community, as a result of reduced payments for medical service from HMOs, hospitals have had to cut their own expenses to the bone just to remain open. Hospitals are being forced to cut back drastically on registered nurses, greatly decreasing the ratio of nurses to patients and replacing many of these RNs with nonprofessionals.

Common sense tells me that the fewer people you have taking care of you, the worse off you are, in one way or another.

This is occurring in San Francisco (and everywhere else), and the board of supervisors' health committee has been working with Local 250 of the Health Care Workers Union to put a halt to health care restructuring in the city until we can get a better handle on what it means. The cause has attracted national attention, and people like Jesse Jackson have joined us in protesting the actions of HMOs. We're especially concerned with the downgrading of staff and the declining quality of care. Janitorial staff, as an example, have been used to perform the functions normally carried out by health care workers—at a fraction of the hourly wage health care workers receive. Health care staff have been expected to perform duties that should be the responsibilities of nurses, and nurses have been taking on doctors' responsibilities—all in an effort to cut costs.

But it's the patients, as always, who pay for these "cost-saving" measures. In one recent instance, a cardiac surgery patient was released from the hospital after only two days and then moved to a convalescent facility, where untrained staff made him perform exercises that directly caused another heart attack. In another, an elderly woman, who, due to nursing cutbacks, could get no response to her calls for assistance, attempted to get to the bathroom on her own, fell out of bed, fractured her skull, and died. In Oakland, a homeless man was examined and discharged from a Kaiser Permanente emergency room with a knife *sticking out of his abdomen*. Incidents such as these are now happening on a regular basis throughout the country.

HMOs that pay for medical care often claim that tens of millions of their members are satisfied with their managed health care. Why shouldn't these people be satisfied? These patients are insured people whose employers pick up the premiums. They usually get good routine care, annual checkups, immunizations for their children, and reminders about upcoming mammograms. These are the measurable "quality" services that HMOs like to brag about in their

134

ads. But the fact is that in any given year, 85% of insured people don't even go to a doctor. This is because most HMO members are employees and their families—in good health—who may need little more than routine health care for years at a time. Ads touting "satisfaction" percentages don't usually include those with serious illnesses like AIDS or cancer.

It's in situations of serious illness that the problems arise. It's when an HMO member faces a costly illness and discovers that he can't get expensive new drugs, a life-saving transplant, or cancer therapy—either because these items are not covered or because they're considered "experimental"—that the real danger of our current health care situation becomes apparent. Patients may even find that they're denied referrals to specialists.

In *Health Against Wealth*, George Anders writes that "managed care, with all its profiteering and inhumane indifference. . .is rapidly becoming the de facto national health policy of the United States." A recent op-ed piece in the *New York Times* said, "Money is being wrung out of health care, as managed-care organizations promised. But it is not being spent to improve medical facilities or for research or better treatment. Much of it is being used to put health care into play on Wall Street, where patients are being traded, sold, merged and brokered for profit like so many pork bellies."

Meanwhile, the managed-care industry continues to blame doctors for the high cost of health care. They say that doctors order too many tests and overtreat. In the past, this certainly was the case; even five years ago we could easily accuse some doctors of profiteering from requiring numerous tests from their own labs or overtreating out of fear of malpractice suits. But this is no longer the situation. In fact, all signs seem to show that undertreatment is now the trend, especially since pre-authorization is required by most managed-care plans for any expensive tests or surgical procedures. In addition, income for doctors has actually declined over the past few years as HMOs have reduced what they'll pay for services. In essence, most doctors have become virtual HMO employees, dependent on the HMO for patients and referrals. They've learned to keep their mouths shut and not complain.

One trend, aimed at preventing doctors from overtreating, has become popular in the industry. Some plans pay doctors a fixed fee per patient each month. This is known as a capitation or per-head payment. This payment is supposedly intended to cover all the costs of providing care for a patient on the plan who selects a particular physician. Supposedly, it prevents doctors from ordering unwarranted tests, referrals, or procedures. At a deeper level, however, capitation and similar physician payment systems serve as financial incentives to doctors to withhold needed care from patients.

Typically, the per-head fee paid to physicians is the same whether an individual on the plan never gets sick or is chronically ill. This works well for doctors if most of their patients are healthy; however, the more referrals a primary-care doctor makes to specialists, or the more tests a doctor orders, the less this doctor retains from the capitation fee. In this way, the unwritten incentive for doctors is to minimize referrals and tests.

The idea of managed care contains an inherent conflict of interest. While companies claim to take care of their members, their financial success requires that they do as little as possible for patients. For-profit organizations are more beholden to their investors than they are to their patients.

Many managed-care companies have come up with an immoral and unethical way to hide the truth about lessened quality of care— the use of "gag rules" to restrict communication between doctors and patients. These rules are imposed on doctors by companies to prevent physicians from telling patients that they might need a more expensive test or treatment than their HMO is willing to provide. In this way, many doctors are prohibited from saying anything critical about a health plan. According to the California Medical Association, perhaps one in five HMOs has such a clause. HMOs argue that gag rules are meant to encourage doctors to discuss their concerns with the company, not with their patients. But many critics assert that physicians are effectively silenced, and that this only works to break down what little communication does exist. It's obvious that gag rules in any managed-care contract should be banned as an infringement on free speech and a breach of doctor–patient trust. At this writing, Congress is considering such a ban.

There are other negative trends at work in the health care industry. One of these relates to mental health coverage, which many plans have begun to limit. Just ten years ago, nearly 8% of money spent on health care went toward the diagnosis and treatment of mental illnesses. And even at that level, care for the mentally ill was greatly underfunded. Today, however, HMOs have cut this amount to 2% or 3%. They are denying adequate hospital care to people who are suicidal, and telling patients that treatment is "not medically necessary" or that they're "not depressed enough" to get treatment. Some HMOs also require the prescribing of less expensive antidepressants instead of more expensive drugs that have fewer side effects. And some have reduced the number of psychotherapy visits a patient can have.

The result is that the insured as well as the uninsured may find themselves in need of community services that have also been cut. Without these services, where are they going to end up if their conditions worsen? I'm not saying that most or many are going to end up on the streets, but there's certainly a relationship between mental health and continued employment. There's also a relationship between unemployment, mental health, and homelessness. And there's certainly a link between mental health, homelessness, and increased expenditures for welfare and other government services.

Managed-care plans also closely control the availability of prescriptions. Nearly 95% of such plans now ask their doctors to prescribe drugs using what they call a "formulary." This is often a list of medications for which the HMO has a discount arrangement with the manufacturer. Many plans require that only drugs from an approved list be prescribed, and HMOs may resist adding expensive new drugs to their formulary, even when there is medical evidence that these medications work better for certain conditions. The idea behind this, of course, is to cut costs. That's why doctors in such plans may tell you that they're going to prescribe a generic drug. Often a formulary can be restrictive, and if a physician prescribes a drug not on the list, the patient must pay the entire cost.

This may not sound all that bad if you're healthy and want to keep your premiums down. But what if you're chronically ill? There are many medical conditions that require patients to pay hundreds of dollars each month just to keep their quality of life intact. One man I knew, Barry, suffered from several AIDS-related conditions for three years before he died. When he was healthy, he'd been a well-off real estate broker. Although his group coverage paid for his hospitalizations and treatments, it never covered the more exotic drugs his doctor prescribed for his particular conditions. These came out of his own pocket to the sum of thousands of dollars during each of those three years.

Although some changes in this area have begun to occur, many others are necessary. In the fall of 1996, President Clinton signed legislation that banned "drive-by deliveries," mandating a two-day minimum hospital stay for women with new babies. Some states have curtailed gag clauses. Moreover, the federal government, under pressure from the American Medical Association and some consumer groups, has rewritten government regulations to require HMOs serving Medicare and Medicaid patients to disclose to the government any payment to physicians of financial bonuses which might discourage patient care. Under the proposed new rules, when such an arrangement might place a substantial portion of a physician's income at risk, plans would be required to protect doctors from excessive financial losses.

The government has been working on these regulations since 1990, but those in the industry have used a variety of tactics to delay implementation of the regulations. Nevertheless, these changes will go into effect. And although they only cover Medicaid and Medicare patients, this is a good start, because about 10% of Medicare and more than 30% of Medicaid patients nationwide are in managed-care plans. The federal rules may also be adopted by states to regulate managed care for patients in the private sector.

Other attempts to regulate health maintenance and managed-care organizations have been discouraging. California voters defeated two November 1996 ballot measures, Propositions 214 and 216, that would have barred gag rules, banned HMOs and managed-care organizations from providing doctors with financial incentives to withhold needed care, and prohibited these organizations from denying services recommended by a patient's doctor unless the refusal was supported by another qualified professional who had examined the patient. Proposition 216 would also have added certain taxes on mergers, acquisitions, and reductions in hospital sizes. In other words, this ballot measure would have tapped those health care profits that have a questionable effect on patient care. Voters, however, were swayed by fear-based advertising that claimed that passage of these initiatives would result in higher premiums and reduced quality of care.

No one knows what causes the many different cancers in this country, but some critics suggest that, in large part, they're a result of environmental toxins, such as those produced by power plants or cigarette smoking. People need to be protected, but political leaders are usually too afraid to do so, because it means upsetting corporate lobbyists who help keep them in power.

I got an early taste of politics in 1969, when I walked down Market Street with my father and Cesar Chavez in support of the grape boycott. My father was the first mayor in the nation to support the farmworkers. The grape boycott and the work of Cesar Chavez were never just about higher wages. They were about pesticides, the health of farmworkers, and women giving birth to deformed children in California's Central Valley. Today San Francisco still supports the farmworkers, mainly because of those same environmental health concerns.

In 1989, my first year in office, I drove to the Central Valley and met many mothers of children with birth defects. There was only one reason for these defects: they were the result of indiscriminate chemical farming for so many years. I told the women that I'd do anything I could in San Francisco to support them and help ensure their safety. Later that year I sponsored legislation to strengthen the position of farmworkers in California with regard to health and safety issues.

There's no excuse for any corporate action that harms children—or anyone else, for that matter. Whether we're talking about tobacco, power plants, cellular antennas, or pesticides, there's no profit-based argument that can justify the destruction either of people's lives or the environment.

The short-term corporate profits are never worth the consequences of disease and enormous health care costs.

In many areas of the country, AIDS is something that afflicts an isolated few; it's not something that affects local politics, decision making, allocation of services, and the hearts and minds of politicians. But in San Francisco, we've been hard hit. We have the highest per-capita rates of AIDS and HIV in the country. But we've also established a standard of care and a range and level of services beyond that of most other communities. Here in the city we've been on the cutting edge of prevention and treatment—we've had to be. We've fought hard to keep AIDS from spiraling more out of control than it already has. We've put up a good fight, and the model we've created for fighting the disease can be put to work elsewhere.

The problem, however, is that the AIDS epidemic is not just a result of HIV; it's also a result of the failure of public officials for the past 15 years to put partisan politics aside and look at the real heart of the issue to find practical solutions. The problem is a two-parter: prevention and treatment. But politics has blindsided those trying to solve the problem.

Though fear and misunderstanding among the public—including those afflicted with the disease—can be blamed for some of the early frustrations of failing to get a handle on AIDS, the Reagan administration and the Republican religious right must bear the overarching burden of our inexcusably slow start in understanding this disease. It's a cliché to point out that had AIDS began by striking straight white men, it would have been eradicated long ago; nonetheless, there's a lot of validity to that argument.

The late writer Randy Shilts identified Patient Zero in the American AIDS epidemic as a gay flight attendant who brought back the disease from Africa or Europe. How might things have been different if a straight flight attendant had been Patient Zero? That one small difference would have changed history and spared the gay population not just the brunt of the epidemic but the forces of hatred and division. The Centers for Disease Control would immediately have received the go-ahead by the Reagan administration, and, as soon as the cause was discovered, nationally authorized prevention programs would have been implemented.

Instead, what we saw was nonresponse. There was a distinct lack of concern because those originally stricken in the U.S. were gay men. They somehow deserved what they got. They brought it on themselves. In less-tolerant religious circles, the "Gay Plague" was no less than God's burning vengeance.

Other than tobacco, the key political issue for me has been HIV and AIDS prevention and treatment. I first became involved with the crisis in the mid-1980s by producing an 18-minute documentary film called "Teens in Focus," about six HIV-positive California teenagers. I'd been doing work with hospices and AIDS groups, and my goal was to make my children and other children understand that this could happen to them. The video, which is still used by the school district, talked honestly about HIV—what it is, how it spreads, and how to avoid it. Back then, it was tough to find six HIV-positive children in Northern California.

Once the causes of HIV became known, the Republican religious right spent years doing everything they could to fight prevention efforts. In particular, they fought AIDS education, especially education about condoms, because this was too close to "sex education," which naturally only makes children want to have sex. As a direct result of lax educational efforts, HIV spread like wildfire into America's heartland. It was not until "innocents"—children like Ryan White—started dying of AIDS that the disease began to get the attention it needed. By then, of course, it was too late to do anything for the tens of thousands of people who might otherwise have been spared.

I recently gave a speech to a group of 800 HIV-positive teenagers in San Francisco. The ten years that have passed since we could hardly find the six to do the video show that we have, as a society, been criminally negligent in trying to remedy the problem.

If we had enacted needle-exchange programs 12 years ago, when we first understood the danger of transmission through drug users' "works," we could have saved untold lives. But such programs were obviously political nightmares. Few politicians had the courage to call for them during Reagan's "war on drugs."

ACT UP, a pivotal AIDS-activism group, were among those who pushed for a locally sanctioned needle-exchange program. With the support of local legislation, the police wouldn't be able to harass people who were handing out syringes, city money could be used to fund the program, an agency could oversee it, and IV drug users—and their sexual partners—could be protected from HIV.

But under Mayor Art Agnos, nothing was being done officially in the city. People responded with vocal protests, especially during the 1991 Gay Freedom Day Parade, when Agnos was campaigning for re-election. In the gay community, needle exchange became an issue in the mayor's race.

When Frank Jordan was elected mayor, I presented my needle-exchange legislation to the board and asked them to declare a state of emergency, which would give the health department the right to sanction needle exchange. That declaration passed, and each month since January 1992, the board has voted to reaffirm the state of emergency.

The rate of HIV transmission among IV drug users has dropped steadily since underground programs were first implemented in early 1987. Nevertheless, you can't fight AIDS by needle exchange alone; you've got to help people get off drugs, and you have to deal with mental health issues that may be tied to high-risk behavior. Whenever I hear about HMOs and managed-care organizations stripping mental health and substance abuse from their coverage, I think about increases in HIV and AIDS and the overall impact on publicly funded budgets across the nation—and on people's lives.

While few politicians have the courage to fight for politically dangerous programs, fewer still are motivated by compassion. Some are truly heartless, placing political posturing above all else—witness California Attorney General Dan Lungren, who has done little to prevent illness and death from HIV and little to ease the burden of pain and nausea for the terminally ill. Lungren has continued, over the years, to threaten San Francisco about our needle exchange program. And recently, when Santa Clara County established its own program, he immediately threatened to send every politician involved to jail. As a result of his "antidrug" and "tough-on-crime" stances, numerous teens and others throughout the state have now been infected with HIV. He's most likely given more people a death sentence from HIV than are housed on death row at San Quentin.

As uncompassionate as Dan Lungren is, California Governor Pete Wilson can make him look like a saint. After I succeeded in getting needle exchange established in San Francisco, a group of us were able to get a needle-exchange bill through the state legislature in 1992—but it was vetoed by Wilson. I immediately introduced board legislation condemning the governor.

The next year the state legislature again passed needle-exchange legislation, and again Wilson vetoed it. So again I introduced a board resolution challenging the governor's veto and his argument. But there is no chance of a program being implemented with Wilson in the statehouse.

The fight now is to get the federal government to approve needle exchange. I have serious doubts about the likelihood of this occurring, though, because of all the political posturing in Washington. Though Clinton has been reelected, his drug "czar," like Dan Lungren, can't appear to be soft on crime. Continuing to posture like this is incomprehensible when lives are at stake.

"Tough-on-crime" posturing by politicians has not only prevented implementation of needle-exchange programs across the country, but it has also prevented those with AIDS, cancer, and other conditions from receiving medicinal marijuana to help ease their suffering.

In May 1989, after my husband Adolfo and I had separated, he got sick with a bleeding ulcer. We soon learned it was stomach cancer. That September, I began taking him to the University of California at San Francisco Medical Center (UCSF) for chemotherapy, which he hated. But he seemed to do well for a while, and even took a trip to Asia the next spring.

One night in June 1990, Adolfo was supposed to take the children and me to dinner, but he never showed up. This was unlike Adolfo. My daughter Angela Mia and I drove down to pick him up, but he didn't answer the door. Angela Mia and I broke into the house and found him. I had never before seen someone who was in so much pain that his teeth were chattering. Although he kept saying he was okay, he couldn't even get out of bed. We got him to the hospital and then finally moved him back to my house.

Adolfo was prescribed medicinal marijuana (then in experimental use) by UCSF doctors that July, and he felt much better that month. He came downstairs to dinner every night. One night the children even took him to Prego restaurant on Union Street for dinner.

But the doctors halted the medicinal marijuana in August, after only a month. They said he had to go back on chemotherapy. They installed an IV pain monitor in his chest so he could receive morphine—Dilaudid—by computer. Adolfo didn't want morphine. He didn't want any pain medicine. Without the marijuana, the pain was so severe he couldn't relax. But the doctors wouldn't give it to him. The Bush administration had taken marijuana off the FDA list, and it was no longer available for testing at UCSF.

Adolfo died on September 5th.

Marijuana was removed from the FDA list because it was an illegal drug. Yet doctors put Adolfo on an opiate, Dilaudid, which is used on the streets as a substitute for heroin. At the time, I figured that they were doctors and they knew what they were doing—and I was in too much emotional pain to put up a fight over it, anyway.

But a year later, what they had done began to dawn on me. That's why I decided to work with former Supervisor Terence Hallinan—now the district attorney of San Francisco—to establish in the city an environment that would be supportive of medicinal marijuana. That's why I've played a role in educating people about the benefits of the drug. That why I sponsored San Francisco Proposition O to decriminalize marijuana for medicinal purposes. That's why I've testified in committee hearings on this, why I've testified in Sacramento, and why I tried to get California and national laws changed. I wrote Clinton to try to get him to change the classification of marijuana from a Schedule I to a Schedule II drug, so that physicians could prescribe it. I was disappointed when the president didn't do a thing about this.

Medicinal marijuana is an issue few politicians will touch. Like needle exchange, people think it can only promote drug use. But in reality, it improves the quality of life for people suffering from glaucoma, cancer, AIDS, anorexia, and other life-threatening illnesses.

Here in San Francisco we have taken a stand. We've passed resolutions in support of medicinal marijuana, and, in the absence of legal changes at the state and federal levels, I authored legislation to decriminalize the sale and possession of marijuana for those with life-threatening illnesses. For years we intentionally allowed marijuana buyers' clubs to remain open, even though marijuana was being openly and publicly sold in storefront locations. Our police were ordered to leave these facilities alone, since they were providing a service to city residents with life-threatening conditions.

In summer 1996, California Attorney General Dan Lungren raided the San Francisco Cannabis Buyers' Club. In response to the club's closing down, a woman with cancer called my office to say that marijuana had helped her through the intense radiation and chemotherapy treatments. The drug had helped her not feel nauseous, so she was able to eat. Her daughter then got on the phone and relayed that her mom was a nice 70-year-old Republican. Those who provide marijuana to the sick and dying aren't harming anyone; they aren't promoting drug use. What they are doing is making some people's lives a bit easier to live—which is more than the politicians have been doing.

Lungren can't possibly give a damn about preventing AIDS, and he certainly can't give a damn about helping to ease the pain of dying people. Not only did he order his troops into San Francisco, but he also used his office as a bully pulpit to fight Proposition 215, the medicinal marijuana initiative. Fortunately, California voters had the wisdom to pass the initiative. And immediately, of course, Dan Lungren and other conservative politicians expressed their outrage.

One HIV-related problem after another seems to materialize as a result of the stalemate in Washington over a coherent AIDS policy. Prevention has been a major problem. But the obstacles to treatment have been even worse. The stalemate began, of course, during the Reagan era. One of the key problems regarding treatment was the failure of the federal government to place AIDS drugs on the FDA-approved list. People who were dying couldn't get the drugs they needed.

I joined a San Francisco group called Project Inform, whose members personally brought in the needed drugs from Mexico. Like many others, I helped them raise money to get whatever drugs they needed. In large part, it was my anger over federal drug policies and the belief that I could make a small difference that helped me decide to run for office in the first place.

Another problem has been bringing local pressure to bear on a national issue. Local issues are often of national significance—requiring national solutions or national assistance—but they don't often lend themselves to photo opportunities. This has been the case with funding for AIDS and HIV. I've gone to Washington several times with my aide, Jerry Windley, to lobby on behalf of AIDS funding. Jerry was a member of ACT UP when we first met. He kept coming to my office with one HIV issue or concern after another, and nearly all of them made perfect sense. After a while, it also made perfect sense to hire him. Together, we've lobbied for increases in funding for the Ryan White CARE Act, for the Housing Opportunities for Persons with AIDS Act (HOPWA), and for research money.

The first year the CARE Act was in effect, it was to receive funding of $188 million. This was reduced to $122 million by the House, and further reduced by the Senate. In San Francisco, which has the largest number of AIDS cases per capita, every dollar counts. So it was important to support increased funding for the CARE Act, because it has meant tens of millions of dollars for us each year.

I met with members of the San Francisco AIDS Foundation and wrote a letter to the mayor urging increased funding. This may sound like an insignificant act, but when a major city complains, the federal government often listens.

This was also the approach we took with HOPWA. Here at the local level we knew how important funding in the area of housing was for those with AIDS—some 10% to 15% of our homeless population is HIV-positive. In 1994, as a result of local pressure here in San Francisco and across the country, the use of HOPWA funds was expanded to include subsidizing apartments and purchasing buildings to house those with HIV.

Nevertheless, some local politicians have failed to understand the hard work and delicate balance that it takes even to receive federal funding. When Frank Jordan was mayor, his planned budget cuts would have dropped us below the minimum "maintenance-of-effort" level of funding that we needed to keep receiving CARE money. As a fiscal conservative, Jordan wanted to cut the budget. But he didn't understand that by cutting small sums of money from our local budget, we nearly lost the $40 million grant that we were getting from the CARE Act. Penny wise and pound foolish. When I saw what was coming, I immediately wrote letters to members of our congressional delegation to warn them and to ask them to intercede with Jordan. It worked in this case, but it hasn't always; in some instances, grants have been lost and services have been cut.

The importance of CARE money has never been lost on me; it provides services to people who can't afford care and who don't have insurance. The beauty of this money is that the only group in the city that has the authority to allocate to and contract with community-based agencies is the CARE Planning Council. The board doesn't; neither does the mayor, although he's the CEO and the appointive officer of the members of the council. For the most part, this means that the money is allocated in nonpolitical ways. It can't be given as a payoff for some political endorsement. The CARE Planning Council has allocated this money wisely, and for the past several years it has prioritized services to primary medical care, housing, transportation, and nutrition.

Like prevention and treatment, housing and the need to integrate AIDS services are problems that are too often ignored. In San Francisco we've been blessed with a number of community-based efforts to help those with AIDS, but many people are too sick or unaware to make the calls and follow up the leads to get the help they need.

Tulio was an Italian immigrant who had been a voice trainer and had worked with several opera stars. His lover died of AIDS in 1989. Tulio was also dying. He and his lover had owned the building in which Tulio was living, but he had had to sell it to pay his lover's estate tax. He sold it with the provision that he could have a lifetime lease on his apartment, but as his health diminished, he wasn't always able to pay his $1,400 monthly rent on time. When the payment was late, the landlord would immediately send him a three-day notice to pay or vacate. To make his rent, Tulio was forced to sell his mementos from his days as an international voice coach. Although the man to whom he sold his building is a gay man with a lover, Tulio got no sympathy from his new landlord.

I received a call from Tulio. He asked me, "Can you think of a way I can get into an apartment? I'm getting kicked out and I'm dying." Fortunately, we were able to set Tulio up with the AIDS Foundation, and they were able to subsidize his rent.

If Tulio was running into problems like this in San Francisco, with its reputation for compassion, then what must it be like for those with AIDS elsewhere in the country? What must it be like in communities without AIDS foundations, or in cities that haven't bothered to apply for federal funds like HOPWA and CARE?

Another issue of critical importance is the problem of obtaining drugs for AIDS treatment. The AIDS Drug Assistance Program (ADAP) is a state-administered program that provides a small number of AIDS medications to people who couldn't otherwise afford them. If a patient's income is below a certain level, he can receive drugs either for free or with a co-payment. ADAP is funded by both state and federal money.

In early 1991, there were only two drugs available on the ADAP list. Even so, the California state health department was considering increasing the co-payment. This was an outrageous proposal—these drugs were keeping people alive, and the people using them couldn't possibly afford a decrease in assistance. For some, a co-payment increase would have been tantamount to a death sentence.

None of the other supervisors at the time took note of the issue. I authored a resolution urging California to continue to provide these two drugs at a reasonable price, to expand the list of drugs covered to more than a dozen, and to not increase the co-payment. The resolution passed and was signed by the mayor.

We got the word out to activists that they needed to start pushing. The troops showed up in force, which brought pressure on the state. I went to Sacramento and testified on behalf of the program. By the end of that year, most of the drugs on our expanded list had been approved.

Since then, AIDS research has identified several new drugs and combinations of drugs that are more effective than their predecessors, making it necessary to keep adding new drugs to the ADAP list. In 1996, researchers at the International AIDS Conference in Vancouver recommended the use of protease inhibitors. These drugs are showing great results in reducing viral load—the amount of HIV in the body. They're keeping people alive much longer, and improving their health and quality of life at the same time. In many cases, people who had severe weight loss and were home on disability when they began taking these drugs have had remarkable weight gains and even returned to work.

But we weren't sure that we'd be able to provide access to the new drugs. In 1996, the state ADAP program had been running a deficit for a year, and people weren't getting the drugs that were already on the list. Knowing the fiscal problems at ADAP, we knew that we needed to make sure that the program was funded adequately by the state, and that ADAP had enough money to add new drugs as they came on line.

The city's department of health services had asked for a $7 million augmentation to ADAP. The board of supervisors passed a resolution supporting the request, urging that three new FDA-approved drugs be added to the list and asking that ADAP be made a line item in the state budget. It hasn't happened as of this writing, but I'm hopeful. And recently President Clinton announced that he was requesting a $65 million increase in federal ADAP funds. If this proposed expenditure gets approved, it should cover the cost here in California.

I believe that people who are sick should have available to them any kind of medicine or herbs that make them feel better. Therefore, I strongly support the Immune Enhancement Project, which provides acupuncture and herbal remedies to people in treatment. The board was able to expand the concept of primary medical care and use CARE money to help pay for these types of service. And the program is cost-effective: if alternative treatments keep these AIDS patients healthy, productive, and out of the hospital, they don't have to go on state aid.

As chair of the health committee, I also introduced a resolution to get the health services board to cover traditional Chinese medicine for city employees. We held a hearing on the issue, and the support for this idea was overwhelming. A huge number of people testified, from patients to Chinese doctors and herbalists, all wanting to share their experiences.

The plan made sense, financially and medically. The insurance rates and the cost of treatment are lower, and the efficacy has been shown to be outstanding. When I first got involved, some people wondered if this was some kind of crackpot scheme. I get that reaction because I'm not afraid to rattle public-policy cages and I'm not afraid of politically dangerous issues like tobacco, needle exchange or medicinal marijuana. When it comes to health and an improved quality of life for people who are dying, there's no time for political business as usual.

I soon had plenty of support for my position. An editorial in the *San Francisco Chronicle* praised me for bringing the issue forward, saying that I was probably "in store for yet another round of 'earth-to-Angela' insults" for my proposal, but that providing coverage for traditional Chinese medical treatments made "considerable sense." The editors added that this should have been done a long time ago. "Far from being a foolish enterprise," they said this proposal showed "the promise of pioneering new ways for consumers and insurance companies to cooperate in keeping people healthier, while holding down costs in our troubled medical care system."

It may take a while, but in the long run I'm often proved right. I think that's because I try to listen to people instead of to lobbyists. It's the people, the local activists, those on the front lines of social issues like AIDS, who have their ears to the ground. If we listen to them, we can learn, and often we can set new and better standards for accessibility to treatment, prevention programs and different health regimens. The way I look at it, it's often the case that as San Francisco goes, so goes the nation. By setting new standards of care here, we can set new standards for the rest of the country.

Knowing what my own battles for AIDS funding have been like here in San Francisco, I can't help but worry about those elsewhere in the country with HIV. I worry about the difficult battle fought by AIDS activists elsewhere, especially in the bible belt. And I worry knowing that a third of Medicaid patients nationwide—including HIV and AIDS patients—have found themselves in a world governed by managed care, where they may not get adequate, up-to-date treatment and the drugs to save their lives.

Because of our AIDS work in San Francisco and the critical problems we've faced here, advocacy groups from Washington have called my office, asking us to write statements and resolutions of support—to put the city on record on national AIDS-related issues. Board resolutions from a city like San Francisco have a serious national impact because they're not simply policy statements. The national attention we get gives us some idea of how powerful a message coming from San Francisco can be. San Francisco, and other cities, can make important statements on national issues when they put a powerful, activist local government on record as supporting an important cause. This can set the tone nationally for the way issues are handled.

One of our resolutions urged the U.S. to drop travel and immigration restrictions on people with HIV. This was motivated in part by our hosting the International AIDS Conference, which many people were prohibited from attending due to federal immigration restrictions on AIDS patients. Because of those restrictions, that conference was the last one held in the U.S.

Resolutions like this tell others throughout the world that we are one of the most welcoming cities anywhere. And they tell people across the country and around the world that "we will not keep you out just because you're sick." They are a powerful tool for setting an agenda and for molding national, and even international, opinion and policies.

I worry because AIDS is still at the bottom of the Abyss.

We're moving toward relegating HIV—currently a fatal, acute disease—to the status of a chronic illness, like diabetes, but we still have a long way to go. It's still something that will kill you. The death rate for AIDS patients is, at this writing, officially 100%. And it's still likely that a large percentage of people who have HIV are going to develop AIDS and die. Better management of the disease means continued funding for people with HIV. And as long as AIDS carries a personal stigma, as long as AIDS is identified as a disease of perverts and degenerates, as long as we have heartless "leaders" in positions of power, that's going to be an uphill fight.

We can't let down our guard. The ebb and flow of state and national politics and the curse of words like "liberal" and "progressive" will be with us for some time to come. Jesse Helms, Pete Wilson, and their ilk keep getting elected and reelected in this country. They ensure that the fight against AIDS is marginalized and fraught with setbacks.

What follows is part of a letter I recently sent to Jesse Helms after he tried once again to block CARE funding:

Your expressions of ignorance and bigotry have helped to win renewed support in the fight against AIDS, especially among the American people and your colleagues in the U.S. Congress. I have made many trips to Washington over the past 7 years to lobby for increased AIDS funding and I have made the reauthorization of the Ryan White CARE Act one of my top priorities. Too many lives have been lost and too many are threatened by this disease. Your blind hatred gives me and many others a reason to fight as hard as we can. Please give my regards to your friends in the tobacco industry. You must be proud to be supporting an industry that woefully misrepresents the health hazards of tobacco to make a profit. You must sleep well at night knowing that you have helped promote cancer, heart disease, and emphysema among the American people. I suppose that's why you have no problem judging and condemning people with HIV and AIDS. If ignorance is bliss, you must be the most contented man in the world.

Helms was kind enough to reply. He argued that we were already spending too much money on AIDS research and treatment, compared to heart disease. "In addition," he continued,

a great deal of Ryan White funds do not even get to innocent victims like the Indiana teenager. Instead the money goes to the pockets of homosexual political advocacy groups. I will not condone spending billions of taxpayer dollars on the promotion of a lifestyle that so many Americans find morally wrong. Of course the growing threat of HIV/AIDS in our society should not be ignored, but to compound the already disproportionate funds with [even more money] is unfair to the many, many Americans who suffer from other, equally dreadful diseases.

155

The shape that Dante saw rising up out of the Abyss has now taken the form of people like Helms.

There will continue to be demonstrations and anger—and deaths—as long as visionless, heartless people are in power. As long as AIDS is seen as a disease of gays, drug users and nonwhite people, as long as the politics of homophobia, sexism and racism play into the AIDS epidemic, it will never receive the attention it deserves.

Politics, prejudice and profits help define the larger issues around health care. As long as health care in this country is rooted in such a profit-based system we're going to have problems. As long as vast sums of money can be made at the expense of the health and even lives of American citizens, the system will fight hard to maintain the dangerous status quo. And as long as we're divided into the haves and have-nots, the crisis of health care—along with crime and homelessness—will continue and undoubtedly worsen.

THE FRAUDULENT:
EVIL COUNSELORS

All ways of winding subtlety I knew,
And with such art conducted, that the sound
Reach'd the world's limit.

INFERNO, CANTO XXVII

MALEBOLGE IS DANTE'S eighth circle of Hell; it is central to the *Inferno*, and Dante devotes 13 cantos to it. The thieves are in the seventh valley or section of the pit, and the evil counselors are in the eighth, even further down and in more torment than the thieves. Among others in the circle is Ulysses, condemned for his role in planning the Trojan horse episode.

Of more interest to us is the presence of a soldier, a man who agrees to tell Dante his story, since he doesn't believe Dante will be able to return from Hell to reveal what he learned. Although the soldier had been cunning as a man of war, he eventually gave up his evil ways and became a monk of Saint Francis's order. But then Pope Boniface VIII called upon the man to devise a plan to make war against other Christians, which the man agreed to do—and so for his trouble sits in Hell, consumed in flames for eternity.

What is a person supposed to do if he or she is called upon to do something unethical by a powerful political figure, a figure the person respects and perhaps admires? What if the person is called upon to do something illegal? What if there is the added incentive of money and power? This is a dangerous combination, and a seductive one. Yet for the typical political consultant, it's just a job description.

In the 1996 presidential race, Bob Dole was widely perceived by the media and the public as having abandoned many of his lifelong beliefs about politics. For example, Dole, who had spent his career arguing in favor of affirmative action and against supply-side economics, suddenly turned 180 degrees on both issues when he decided he wanted to be president more than anything. He also selected Jack Kemp as his running mate, a man with whom he had never gotten along and in whose economic theories he never believed.

Did Bob Dole have a sudden, conservative change of heart? Of course not. He was acting on the bad (in his case) advice of political consultants. Handlers. Spin doctors. Whatever name the press gives them, they are the people who pull the strings behind any political candidate at any level. They conduct polls, orchestrate campaign themes, shape and reshape their candidates, execute dirty tricks against opposing candidates whenever necessary, and sometimes stay on after an election to secretly flip the switches of office.

In American politics, operatives are a necessary evil, but they pose a serious problem to the democratic process. Because of the sheer number of candidates they often must simultaneously manage, they are often dependent on political machines to secure their own economic fortunes and to secure the "best" candidates for all-important victories—victories that ensure the value of the high fees they charge to other candidates. As a result, outsiders and other independents can have trouble even hiring an able consultant, and, again, democracy is the loser.

To bring about a political victory, consultants follow their own rules. They'll do anything to get their candidate elected. *Anything.* They have a short-term memory problem when it comes to loyalty to former candidates. And they often work behind the scenes with machines—even, perhaps, against the candidates whom they're supposedly trying to get elected.

The lack of honor and loyalty among many political consultants can be seen in the case of Dick Morris, the former consultant and advisor to President Clinton. In a story that first broke in the *Star*, a supermarket rag, during the week of the 1996 Democratic National Convention, Sherry Rowlands, a prostitute, revealed diary entries that said Morris had shared White House information with her during their encounters in a Washington hotel. She claimed that to impress her, Morris allowed her to listen to calls he made to President Clinton on a private line at the White House, read her portions of the vice president's acceptance speech, and made disparaging remarks about the president and first lady—the same president whom he had helped elect and for whom he had worked off and on for nearly two decades.

On first glance, this story appears to be about little more than the rise and fall of a man with a big mouth and an even bigger ego. But the story doesn't end here. If it did, it would not take into account the genius of a political consultant like Dick Morris—a man who was the architect for Bill Clinton's presidential bid; who took Clinton from the Arkansas statehouse to the White House; and who engineered Clinton's shift to the political center, including persuading the president to adopt a pseudo-Republican welfare-reform package.

Some "coincidences" need to be examined. The story broke the same week that Morris's photo graced the cover of *Time* and the same day that President Clinton delivered his acceptance speech at the convention, guaranteeing a national news audience for the story. It broke at the same time Morris was in negotiations with Random House on a book deal. And it probably guaranteed another *Time* cover for Morris, national publicity and money for Rowlands, and a final book contract for Morris of $2.5 million. The disclosure meant that Morris was not a man on his way down and out, but on his way to fame and financial success.

Some coincidences.

The Morris–Rowlands story illustrates several political truths. It shows the power that political consultants can have in shaping public policy and dictating legislation. By capturing the president's ear and promoting welfare reform behind the scenes, Morris—a man never elected to public office and not accountable to voters—was able almost single-handedly to reverse 60 years of federal policies toward the poor, policies that had begun in the 1930s under FDR and were enhanced by Lyndon Johnson's War on Poverty in the 1960s. Is this how we should go about reforming welfare?

From the way they use their power to strategize, it's clear that some political consultants are interested only in getting their bosses elected and reelected and, in doing so, keeping themselves in positions of power—even if it means our leaders' waffling over issues of ideological integrity.

The Morris story also shows the lack of loyalty that political consultants feel to anyone other than themselves. Not only might a single consultant work for both Democrats and Republicans, liberals and conservatives—often at the same time—but few have qualms about using inside information about former bosses to help elect their new bosses. During the 1992 primaries, before Morris went back to work for Clinton, some say that he revealed information about what would become the Gennifer Flowers fiasco.

If Morris is any example, some consultants will sell out anyone if the price is right. In Morris's case, it appears that $2.5 million was just about the right price. And he's not the only one, of course. I have no idea what the size of Ed Rollins's publishing advance was, but according to his own book, *Bare Knuckles and Back Rooms*, Rollins had a similarly easy time switching his allegiance from Reagan and Bush to Perot in 1992. He also dedicates a significant portion of his book to bashing former clients and their wives.

Some may say that politics is only another form of business, and that political consultants are merely selling their services to the highest bidder. If that's the case, then business must be good.

Political consultants will do anything to get their candidate into office. This often means uncovering dirt against opposing candidates and, where there's too little dirt to uncover, using negative campaigning and dirty tricks to create their own. We need look no further than Bill Clinton and Gennifer Flowers or Hillary Clinton and Whitewater. If Gennifer Flowers or Whitewater didn't exist—

and the public still knows almost no real facts about either case—political operatives would have created them.

I knew next to nothing about political consultants when I first ran for political office in 1986. I did know that they were necessary for victory and planned all aspects of a campaign. I soon learned that a political consultant tells you where to be and when, how to focus your energy, and what to say and what *not* to say. Some political consultants, however, go far beyond this. Over the years I learned that they're the masters of dirty campaigns and, when they serve higher masters or feel slighted, have little loyalty to the candidates for whom they once worked.

During my first run for the board in 1986, I hired Richie Ross, who had a reputation as a first-rate political consultant. I had met him in 1985 in the home of Willie Brown's girlfriend. During that campaign, Ross orchestrated a nasty, mean-spirited campaign that unfairly targeted incumbent Supervisor Wendy Nelder's integrity and sanity. The attack was brutal, but I still lost.

Ross was the first consultant with conflicting agendas I came up against. He was the first to show me—through example—the evils of the political industry and the overarching loyalty that some have only to themselves. I saw this more clearly in 1988.

I discovered that Ross had been serving other masters: Brown and the machine. He was Brown's chief of staff when Brown was Speaker of the Assembly and was later appointed by Brown as director of majority services; that is, he was in charge of the re-election campaigns of all the Democratic state legislators.

I now believe that Ross wanted to remove Nelder as a favor to Brown. He didn't succeed. Whatever his motives, he certainly wasn't interested in serving me, in developing a campaign that reflected my own personality and feelings about people and issues. Instead of following my own intuition, I paid him hundreds of thousands of dollars, because I'd been told that he knew what he was doing.

My bid for election in 1986 served another purpose for Ross than merely making money. It also served multiple purposes for the machine. In addition to trying to get Wendy Nelder out of the way for Brown, I now believe, Ross came down from Sacramento to run my campaign to help cultivate the city for Art Agnos in his mayoral bid the following year. Using my campaign as an organizing tool, he was able to garner the support of my backers for Agnos in 1987.

In 1988, I again ran for supervisor, and I expected that the consulting team of Richie Ross and Larry Tramatola would work on my campaign. After all, they had promised, and I had helped them through my efforts on the Agnos campaign. But after the Agnos victory, Agnos and his manager Ross no longer needed me. And when it had become clear that I wasn't part of the machine, Ross and Tramatola withdrew. The excuse Ross gave me was that he hadn't been paid; in fact, he had been *overpaid*.

By this time it was almost too late for me to run. The campaigns for the other supervisorial candidates were in high gear, and most of their finance committees were already in place collecting funds. At the last minute, Kevin Shelley stepped in to help plan my campaign and arranged for me to hire the team of Michael Ganley and Michael Terris.

I won in 1988 because I had learned from my 1986 campaign. This time I followed my heart, and I mastered the field operation necessary for getting people out on the streets, walking precincts, and passing out flyers. I was out at the bus stops at 6:15 every morning, talking to people.

In 1991, when I joined the mayor's race at the last minute, I hired the team of Michael Terris and Eric Jaye. Like me, they were not a part of the machine. Unlike Ross, they were honest and loyal.

A great deal of the blame for my losing that race belongs to the dirty tricks that Ross used against me. In managing Agnos's campaign, Ross turned the $250,000 I'd advanced him against me, accusing me of not having paid taxes on it. Ross knew what money I had taken in during my 1986 campaign. He knew that the fee on which I had taken the advance wasn't due until 1992. He knew that the advance was not a taxable event until the fee came in. Nevertheless, my former consultant had me investigated by the IRS and the Fair Political Practices Commission (FPPC) just three weeks before the election. He also had me investigated by the FPPC on complaints that I had failed to disclose the value of a mailer sent on my behalf by the San Francisco Police Officers' Association. Although these created devastating headlines in the last few weeks of the campaign, in January the FPPC gave me a clean bill of health. The IRS reviewed the $250,000 advance and found no wrongdoing.

By the time all the smoke blew away, of course, the election was over.

The pressure on me was enormous during that campaign, and I believe it was all engineered by Richie Ross. He had taken the money in 1986 knowing that I was going to lose, and then he had used the money issue against me in 1991.

In early 1992, I needed to begin preparations for my fall re-election bid for the board of supervisors. We had just finished the mayoral campaign when Eric Jaye called me. This was just after I'd been beaten up in the newspapers and had lost the mayor's race, and I remember him asking me, "How do you get up in the morning?" Even with all that I had been through, I was still optimistic. However, I felt that Jaye and Terris were fed up with the job, so I didn't rehire them for the 1992 race.

This was a mistake on my part. I felt that "inconveniences" like baseless investigations, disloyal consultants, and political defeat shouldn't stand in my way. So what did I do? I hired Jack Davis, whom I had met a few months before, and who had successfully run Frank Jordan's mayoral campaign. Jack had been politically courting me, and he had a large field operation in place from the previous fall.

Davis is streetwise and dangerous when slighted. I may have won re-election and the board presidency by a substantial margin, but I lost Terris and Jaye in the process—a reality I will always regret.

The one thing I eventually learned from all this was never to drop a consultant who is honest and loyal. They're too rare. Honesty is more important than aggressiveness. And a positive campaign—even an unsuccessful one—is better than a victorious negative campaign; the latter is bad for the soul.

Political victory can still be achieved—with luck and money—by focusing on issues rather than on personal attacks.

I'm no stranger to the creation of scandal and the manipulation of facts by political consultants and hungry journalists looking to sell newspapers. I have experienced my own Willie Horton in the form of an insidious campaign against me because of a friendship I had with a person who, I discovered later, was a con man. The media picked up on it, and, while the man involved ended up in jail for what he did, I learned a tough lesson about political realities.

During the spring and early summer of 1993, I was at the height of my political popularity. I had been elected the previous November as president of the board of supervisors. During the previous two and a half years, I had refused to play ball with the machine against my friend Jerry Brown, I had helped to defeat Agnos, I had stood up to Mayor Jordan's police tactics following the Rodney King "riots," and I was now publicly and vehemently opposing Jordan's Matrix program.

In June, even before Jordan's Matrix program was put in place, I had hired David Binder to conduct a field poll. He found that I would place first—by almost two to one—against my nearest contender in a race for mayor. The poll matched me against Jordan, Assemblyman John Burton, assembly Speaker Willie Brown, and Supervisor Carole Migden. The machine was scared, and Jack

Davis—who always wanted a winning ticket, and who was feuding with Jordan—was looking for his next mayoral campaign.

When the poll was released, I got a call from Jack, who wondered if I knew what the poll numbers meant. I knew Jack well by that point—he had run my campaign for board president—but he was hardly my best friend. Nevertheless, it offended him that he hadn't been consulted about the poll. He appeared to be even more offended when I didn't take him up on his offer to meet to discuss the poll results. But the 1995 mayor's race was two years away and I still considered myself independent. I didn't want to be managed.

Although the machine had kept up its efforts to discredit me politically, by June 1994, everyone knew that I was planning to run for mayor in 1995, and I was still the most popular potential candidate. I was the most popular potential candidate, that is, until the media linked me to the con man, and until I put off Jack Davis one too many times.

From the summer of 1994 on, the attacks against me picked up steam. The headlines suggested I'd been wined and dined and flown to New York on stolen money—a flat-out lie. That I'd used poor judgment. The media was having a field day, and it looked like the machine was going to make sure I wasn't the next mayor of San Francisco.

There are no coincidences.

If it seems like every political figure who has been through the ringer sounds paranoid, there's a good reason why: people are always after your job. You are also always after someone else's job, and that someone else wants desperately to hang on to that job. It's not merely "Angela's paranoia" to draw connections between media stories and my political enemies. Such things are as common as fireflies on a summer night, as Dante might say.

Who had a vested interest in my losing the mayoral race? My opponents, of course: we all wanted the same job.

But who pulls the strings of the candidates?

Richie Ross seems a likely suspect. But he's not the only one.

Jack Davis had always been antagonistic towards Mayor Art Agnos. In 1991, he served as Frank Jordan's consultant at least partially because he wanted to end Agnos's career in revenge for Agnos's having him indicted over a ballpark financing scam some years earlier. The next year, 1992, he readily served as my consultant, but felt rebuffed when I put him off in discussing the next mayoral race. By the summer of 1994, after my opposition to the city's contract with Motorola—and Davis's loss of a huge commission as Motorola's lobbyist—I perceived that he was actively working to destroy my political career.

After being rebuffed by Jordan, Jack decided to go after both him and me. At the least he would seek another mayoral candidate to manage in 1995. First, he asked Carole Migden to run. When that failed he asked Kevin Shelley. Finally, he convinced Brown. Jack told me that it had taken him eight months to find someone to run.

He told me, "You blew it, Angela. I could have made you mayor. Now I'm going to make Willie mayor instead." Well, with the help of three million bucks in Brown's campaign war chest, at any rate.

Jack Davis, because of hate, has taken down two mayors and created two. Not only did he create Jordan, he also destroyed him. He once told me that he *didn't* spend his days and nights thinking about ways to ruin people. I thought it was an odd thing to say at the time, but now I understand: the consultant doth protest too much, methinks.

Though he remembers it differently, I first met Jack in September 1991, during one of the mayoral debates. As I walked by, he reached out and said, "Angela, I'm Jack Davis. I can't tell you how honored I am to meet you." Although I was Jordan's opponent, it struck me that he was not saying this to Angela the candidate, but to Angela the San Franciscan, the daughter of Joe Alioto, the supervisor fighting for AIDS services. I felt it was a gesture of honest, genuine respect. He later told me, however, that he'd had me investigated and so felt as if he already knew me. He said that he had even sent his people out to the Convent of the Sacred Heart, where I had attended school back in the late 1960s. He said, "I can't find anything against you." This told me a lot about Jack Davis. It's also a little disheartening that personal investigations have become second nature to me.

Other incidents that occurred in the 1995 mayoral race looked like the work of Richie Ross. As in 1991, I was being investigated by the FPPC. Although it was conveniently overlooked by the *Daily Journal*, which reported the original story, and their lightweight reporter, the FPPC responded to these allegations by noting that the previous investigation by the district attorney had given me a clean bill of health.

In a recent phone call, Jack Davis pointed out that Ross had accused me of being a criminal, tried to put me in jail, and had me investigated by the FPPC. When I hung up the phone, I wondered: Was Jack innocent in all of this? Did he merely stand by and watch Ross in action?

Or was he capable of orchestrating a political attack of this magnitude? Unquestionably.

This chapter is the one that people may have thought I wouldn't write. A lot of people will probably turn to it first, and some might not read any farther. They may be disappointed that I didn't name all the names I might have.

I have sometimes exercised bad judgment in my life, there is no question of that. I've made decisions, some good, some bad. We all do that in life. The media and the political machine wouldn't have much ammo to fire at me if I hadn't.

But the media and the machine are responsible for setting some of that ammo in my path, like land mines. And you can't always see every land mine. I stepped on some, just like anyone would. Bill Clinton steps on them all the time. Even Willie Brown steps on one now and again, such as referring, in the *New Yorker,* to the San Francisco Board of Supervisors as "pantywaists" and "mistresses that need servicing."

The heart of the matter is that, as a woman and as a foil to the political machine, I've been a prime target. Any politician who sets herself up as an independent alternative to the status quo faces similar pitfalls. So while I take responsibility for my part in the success of evil counselors in bringing a Trojan horse of scandal to my front door, the fact remains that we all must keep an eye out for the machinations of political operatives. They are the ones who decide who will have the power in our "democracy."

THE FRAUDULENT:
THIEVES WITH CITY HALL
IN THEIR POCKETS

Amid this dread exuberance of woe
Ran naked spirits wing'd with horrible fear,
Nor hope had they of crevice where to hide,
Or heliotrope to charm them out of view.

INFERNO, CANTO XXIV

T HE DEEPER DANTE DESCENDS INTO HELL, the worse off are the souls of the damned, and the more terrifying the demons and dangers he encounters; horror movies have nothing on Dante for gore. Across the sixth chasm of the seventh circle, Dante leads his readers into a terrible place where gangs of demons eternally disembowel and otherwise rip up those who, in life, sold out the trust placed in them. One spirit, a man who had been in the service of a king, is condemned to be forever rent by demons with hooks for selling political favors for money.

In the next chasm, the thieves of this world are eternally consumed by serpents. Dante was writing of petty thieves mostly, but there are bigger thieves out there. A man who steals money from the public under the guise of public service is as guilty of thievery as a man who breaks into a jeweler's and steals a diamond.

We've spent words and pages and chapters dancing around the central, unasked question raised by this book: what exactly makes politics go?

The fires of Hell are fueled by dollar bills.

In a recent *San Francisco Chronicle* op-ed response to an unfavorable article on the gambling industry's lobbying, a representative of the gambling firm Ladbroke hit the nail on the head. His phrasing was subtle, but his allusion to a "democracy which encourages financial participation" was clear. I'm not as subtle: it costs money to play politics. I'm not referring to federally regulated campaign contribution maximums, either—a major portion of legislative energy is devoted to creatively sidestepping campaign contribution laws. I'm talking about the millions of dollars a day that flow into political coffers.

This is an explosive issue. Ordinary citizens have become outraged at the piles of money thrown at candidates by industry. The topic of campaign-finance reform is bandied about by politicians as a "problem," then deliberately obscured, and finally ignored altogether. In the 1996 presidential campaign, we had two contenders and their handlers flinging around accusations that the other guy's party was kowtowing to "special interests." Dole accuses Clinton of accepting half a million bucks from an Indonesian business dynasty; Clinton points out that Dole took money from the same people.

Pot, meet kettle.

The Motorola case is not sexy. It's nothing out of the ordinary. Similar events go unnoticed every day at the local, state, and federal levels—and that's exactly why it's important. On the surface it's a simple story of a company being awarded a contract to provide services to a city. A closer look, however, suggests political paybacks, collusion, and perhaps even an explanation for the continued high cost of government. Politicians talk about cutting costs and complain about the high price tag for social services, but these are often the same officials who participate in private giveaways of public contracts to their friends. And when I say "giveaways," I'm not talking about garden-variety pork-barrel politics; I'm talking about influence peddling in essential contracts and the delivery of vital services.

In June 1994, San Francisco voters approved a bond measure calling for the allocation of $40 million for a state-of-the-art radio system that would link fire, police, paramedics, and several other city agencies. The following October, the city's chief administrative officer (CAO), who oversees purchasing, authorized the city's department of electricity to enter into negotiations with Motorola to supply the services.

Instead of soliciting bids, as is required under the city's charter for projects costing more than $5,000 (or $50,000 in a few specific cases), the CAO approved a sole-source contract with Motorola. As he explained it, the city had already purchased some $4.8 million worth of Motorola radio equipment that would all have to be scrapped if the contract was awarded to another supplier. This explanation notwithstanding, the contract clearly violated the city's competitive-bidding requirement.

I was outraged at what appeared to be a lack of common sense. If I won't walk into a store and plunk down $40 for a clock radio without doing at least a little comparison shopping, I wasn't going to let the city toss away $40 *million*. It was incomprehensible to me to allow a $4.8 million tail to wag a $40 million dog, especially when a competitive bid might save far more than the initial equipment investment. I wouldn't spend an extra 20 bucks on a clock radio just because my extension cord only fits a certain model.

The basic rule is that competition in any bidding process is not only healthy but usually results in lower bids and higher efficiency by the winning company. In fact, until the CAO made his announcement, another company, Ericsson GE, had made it known that it was ready to bid on the project.

I was further outraged because the Motorola deal was being lobbied at city hall by Jack Davis, who not only had run Frank Jordan's campaign in 1991 but was now serving as his political consultant. If his lobbying efforts were successful, Davis would undoubtedly receive a percentage of that $40 million. This was a clear conflict of interest. But as strange as it seems, there were no rules to restrict a mayor's political advisor from also working as a lobbyist.

When I brought my complaint before the board, I enjoyed strong support. Yet six days later, my attempt to force the city to put the contract out to bid was defeated in a seven-to-one vote.

Someone was making some phone calls.

No one on the board acknowledged evidence of wrongdoing or of Jack Davis's potential influence over the mayor or CAO, but the *San Francisco Examiner* editors decided the truth needed reporting. They subtitled an editorial, "San Francisco Supervisors See No Point in Saving Millions." In it they argued that there was only one explanation why Motorola was awarded the contract: "Motorola's lobbyist is Jack Davis. . . .The devil in Jack Davis is said to strike fear in the hearts of timorous supervisors." The *Examiner* pointed out that since engineering Jordan's victory in 1991, Davis had made hundreds of thousands of dollars as both a political advisor and a lobbyist with "unfettered access to the mayor."

After the vote, I urged Motorola's competitor, Ericsson GE, to consider seeking a court injunction because of the illegal contract. They did so; a federal judge signed the injunction. And later, in 1995, a San Francisco court indeed found the sole-source contract to be illegal. In the summer of 1996, the city finally solicited bids.

I've learned two things in political life: victory is never certain, and there are no coincidences. There's always another rug to be pulled out from under someone. In this case, three "unrelated" events occurred. First, newly elected Mayor Willie Brown, whose campaign was managed by Jack Davis, announced that he still supported Motorola's quest for a sole-source contract. Then it was discovered that the radio system specifications, compiled by the department of electricity, included at least 40 different pieces of equipment that were made only by Motorola. Ericsson GE, which had built radio systems for Los Angeles and other cities, argued that its own systems and equipment were more than adequate. One expert I called in from Stanford said, "If you don't set specifications that can be addressed by multiple suppliers, you're going to discourage competition." This should have been obvious to anyone, but the city officials behind the deal clearly had their own agenda.

On the heels of these revelations, the city's own foreign policy was used against Ericsson GE. In 1996, the board of supervisors passed legislation requiring the city to boycott companies doing business in Burma. As it turned out, both Motorola and Ericsson GE had ties to Burma. Motorola had about a million dollars' worth of business there, and Ericsson LM, the European parent company of Ericsson GE, owned a Burmese subsidiary. Although Ericsson GE had no direct connection with Burma, and our law had an escape clause for lower bids, a board of supervisors' vote would be required. Before we could act, however, Motorola quickly canceled its small Burma contracts. Who wouldn't be willing to sacrifice a million dollars for the multiple millions a San Francisco contract would be worth?

Ericsson GE dropped out of the bidding then, presumably because of the Burmese subsidiary. As of this writing, the issue has not been resolved. A law requiring political consultants to disclose their activities and finances, the first of its kind in the nation, was passed by the board of supervisors in October 1996—and vetoed by Brown. We initially had enough votes to override this veto, but as the money and influence started spreading around, seven of the supervisors changed their minds and decided not to fight the mayor.

When Motorola is awarded the contract, as I have every reason to believe it will be, all the players involved—the mayor, his consultant/Motorola's lobbyist, and Motorola itself—will have cheated San Francisco out of $14 million—the amount the city would have saved had Ericsson GE's bid been submitted and approved.

That $14 million would have paid for a lot of AIDS clinic workers.

Or homeless shelters.

Or prenatal care for poor women.

Or library books.

Does anybody think this isn't robbery?

How common are cases like the Motorola one? In 1994, two weeks after the initial sole-source contract was issued, I called the head of purchasing for the city and asked how many contracts over $50,000 had been awarded over the previous two years without competitive bids, based on sole-source exemption. In response, I was sent on a month-long wild goose chase. Finally, after threatening to subpoena the entire city purchaser's office, I was given a list of the contracts.

The total value of the contracts was over $700 million. One contract, worth nearly $100 million, was for an excavation—a *hole*—at the end of Market Street.

One. Hundred. Million. Dollars. There was no way *that* figure was the result of competitive bidding. For a tenth of that amount, I'd walk down Market Street with a spoon and dig the damn thing myself.

The potential for corruption in awarding these contracts is enormous and is a facet of government that nobody has bothered to investigate. In talking with investigative journalists about it, I've been told, "It's too big to go after; it's out of control." This one list covering just two years represented nearly three-quarters of a billion dollars in one small city. If you use the Motorola contract as a basis for calculating the amount of overbidding, you come up with a percentage of 35. We can infer, then, that sole-source contracts are inflated by about 35%. Some will be more, some less. Add that up nationwide, and throw in the federal government. What could this nation accomplish with that kind of money?

My fight against the Motorola contract was another reason why Jack Davis went to war against me, why I was viciously attacked by the machine, and why I was subjected to harassment in my 1995 and 1996 campaigns in the form of various investigations by the police, the district attorney's office and the FPPC. As a footnote, you should know that there were *two* bond measures in the 1994 election. The first one, the $40 million one, was for only the initial implementation of emergency radio services for the city. The company awarded the first contract was practically guaranteed to get the second contract, worth up to $60 million. I assume Motorola's lobbyist—Jack Davis—would have been due a commission on this second contract as well.

In late 1994, I requested that the recently formed ethics panel bar political consultants from also serving as lobbyists. My efforts were labeled vindictive and personal, and nothing resulted from them. Two years later a colleague, Supervisor Tom Ammiano, introduced legislation that would have addressed this issue by prohibiting anyone who had done a certain amount of campaign work from lobbying any city official, commissioner, or employee, even if he had not worked on that particular person's campaign. This effort was attacked as an affront to free speech and, though it passed the board, it was vetoed by Brown, who is not well known as a champion of free expression.

Politics and business are intimately linked. No matter how much we'd like to believe that issues and contracts are decided simply on their merits, they're not. And no matter how much political leaders talk about the bottom line, there's a secret layer of influence that lies between cost and contract. This layer includes lobbyists, who get the job in the first place because of their friendships with elected officials and bureaucrats. So retired generals represent the defense industry. The former secretary of education works the anti-education factions in Congress. But the Motorola case shows that this layer includes people who are more than just lobbyists. It includes people who hold the futures of individual politicians in their hands.

This is not about Motorola as an organization. The issue was never about quality or service—Motorola has a reputation as a top-flight company. Its managers don't even let the bottom line dictate all their policies: to help prevent mass civilian deaths in Bosnia and other areas of conflict, the company recently stopped providing electronic components to companies that manufacture land mines. Nor am I saying that Jack Davis has ever broken a conflict-of-interest law. He's used his genius to elect politicians and then has held that fact over their heads—and his political influence makes it difficult to pass such a law. But whether it's because of that secret shared power or because of the fear that such genius might be turned against them, the effects are the same. That's politics.

There are others who also occupy this layer of influence. These are the corporations that have historical power in a region, and that may have wielded a corrupting influence for decades. A lot of us want to believe that influence peddling disappeared earlier in the century, and that laws are now firmly in place to prevent the misuse of influence exposed by Upton Sinclair and other muckrakers. Maybe so. But the massive political influence of the giants of industry have not gone the way of the land and railroad barons of history. And such historical political influence still exists at the local level. In fact, it exists nearly everywhere, and in San Francisco its name is Pacific Gas and Electric—PG&E.

The effect of PG&E's influence in San Francisco has been far greater than merely controlling elections and politicians for corporate gain. Though PG&E has done this with great finesse, the real impact of its political control has been to rob the city of hundreds of millions of dollars over most of this century. It has done this by using whatever means it has felt necessary to prevent the city from taking control of its own electrical power—as was originally required by a 1913 federal law (the Raker Act) and a 1939 U.S. Supreme Court decision—and, I believe, by defrauding the city of tens of millions of dollars in potential fees for delivering electrical power to its customers. The most horrific aspect of this fraud has been the complicity of city politicians at every step along the way.

The story begins before the 1906 San Francisco earthquake, when the Spring Valley Water Company held a monopoly to provide water to the city. With population growth it became apparent that a new citywide water system was needed, one with adequate water supplies. However, a new sense of urgency materialized with the devastating fires—which were partly the result of Spring Valley's cheap construction—following the 1906 earthquake. Searching for additional water sources, the city found the Hetch Hetchy Valley in Yosemite National Park and devised a plan to dam the valley and pipe the water the 189 miles to San Francisco.

The plan was finally approved in 1913 when Congressman John Raker introduced legislation to let San Francisco build the dam. The conditions, which have been in effect since then, state that the dam must also be used to generate electricity, which then must be sold directly to the citizens at the lowest possible rates through a municipal power agency. The Raker Act also states that if the city fails to meet these requirements, the Hetch Hetchy grant reverts to the federal government.

After the dam was completed in 1923, the city revoked its franchise to Spring Valley for water and created its own municipal water system. It also began building transmission lines to carry power to the city, but in 1925 it ran out of money, conveniently, just a few hundred yards away from a PG&E substation and high-voltage cable. As a "temporary" measure, the city decided to sell Hetch Hetchy power to PG&E at wholesale; PG&E would then sell the power to its San Francisco customers at retail. PG&E paid the city a small franchise fee for use of city streets and easements and pocketed the profits on the retail cost of the electricity.

This marked the beginning of PG&E's takeover of San Francisco power and of a 70-year violation by the utility and city officials of the conditions of the Raker Act. In 1927, San Francisco supervisors

181

placed a bond measure on the ballot to buy the equipment needed to establish municipal power. PG&E vehemently fought the measure, which failed. At that point the federal government stepped in, demanding that the city enforce the Raker Act. Another bond measure was placed on the ballot, and again PG&E was successful, convincing voters that the bond measure and municipal power would raise taxes. This happened time and time again over the years, until a federal judge ruled that the city's contracts with PG&E violated the Raker Act's ban on the sale of power to a private corporation. In 1939, the U.S. Supreme Court upheld this ruling.

As was typical for the era, both the *San Francisco Chronicle* and the *Examiner* ran editorials on behalf of PG&E and against the Supreme Court ruling. For the next several years the battle between the federal government and the city over the PG&E contracts continued. It's been a story of failed bond measures, attempts by the federal government to enforce compliance, delaying tactics by city officials in implementing public power, and multidecade contracts with PG&E. In 1972, a group of pro bono CPAs, Accountants for the Public Interest, conducted a study and discovered that the city could profit by $22 million annually, after costs, by buying out PG&E service in San Francisco and municipalizing the delivery of power to city residents. The next year, a civil grand jury investigated the Raker Act and the city's contracts with PG&E and concluded that public power was required by law. Nothing came of it.

Finally, in 1982, a citizens' group known as San Franciscans for Public Power was able to place an initiative on the ballot calling for a study of the feasibility of public power. This measure was defeated after PG&E spent more than $600,000 to oppose it, with the help of then-Mayor Dianne Feinstein. With the specter of a feasibility study out of the way, PG&E immediately attempted to raise the rates that it charged the city both for use of PG&E's power lines to provide the city's own power to public buildings and for backup of the city's power supply when low water levels cut the city's power production at Hetch Hetchy.

In late 1987, Mayor-elect Art Agnos, who'd formerly been pro-public power, was summoned by PG&E head Dick Clarke, who told Agnos that the contracts with PG&E could not be discontinued and that PG&E had all the votes it needed on the board of supervisors to prevent public power in San Francisco. According to *The San Francisco Bay Guardian*, Agnos was also told that if he didn't want to play ball, PG&E would "crush his political career." The next year, the *Guardian* released its own analysis, in which it found that the city was losing more than $150 million each year to PG&E by failing to comply with the Raker Act and establish a municipal utility. Later that year the board voted eight to three to go along with PG&E for the next 27 years, even though this agreement—like all the contracts that have preceded it—is in violation of federal law. Agnos, perhaps seeing the political writing on the wall, signed the contract. This occurred even after the city's budget analyst reported that the contracts were a bad deal, and a violation of standard city procedures, even going so far as to recommend that the supervisors oppose the contracts.

I became actively involved in the public power debate soon after I took office and, with then-supervisor Terence Hallinan, co-authored a resolution allocating $50,000 for the long-sought-after feasibility study. It passed and was to become effective in early 1991. Agnos wouldn't sign the resolution, nor did he include the funding for it in the 1992–1993 budget. The study was never performed. As had been the case since 1927, PG&E was behind the scenes, killing the effort.

In 1994, as president of the board, I established a select committee of the board on the municipalization of public power. I then made a motion for $150,000 to produce a feasibility study on the municipalization of power. The vote was seven to three in favor but, as Art Agnos had done before him, Frank Jordan refused the funding. This time we didn't even have the eight votes necessary to override his refusal.

The next year, 1995, I decided to try again. This time I authored an ordinance modifying the administrative code to require the Public Utilities Commission (PUC) to "author and submit to the board by June 30, 1996, a report regarding the feasibility of municipalizing the city's utilities distribution system in San Francisco." The ordinance also stated that "willful failure to discharge such duties would be deemed official misconduct." Again I included a request for $150,000 for the study. This time, the ordinance was approved by the board on an eight-to-two vote. The mayor refused to sign it, but the ordinance became law in April. Even though a feasibility study performed for Chicago had cost over a million dollars, this small figure of $150,000 was the best we could do. In a coincidental twist of fate, however, this request for supplemental allocation, which left the controller's office on May 12, took 11 days to reach the mayor's budget director—five days too late to be included in the city's 1995–1996 budget. Obviously, the long trip between two offices in the same building was fraught with unforeseen hazards.

I was so angry that I made a board motion to add $150,000 back to Hetch Hetchy's budget and shift those funds to pay for the feasibility study. With an eight-to-three vote in favor of my motion, the mayor's support was unnecessary, and the study could finally move forward.

The PUC had voted repeatedly to oppose any funding for a feasibility study. It was only after the board passed legislation requiring a study that the PUC reluctantly complied, and issued a request for proposals from independent consultants.

When the bids came in, the PUC scored the competing consultants on a number of categories. These numbers were then tallied, and the bidder with the highest score was to be awarded the contract. When the PUC revealed its final choice, it was discovered by *The San Francisco Bay Guardian* and San Franciscans for Public

Power that the contract was being given to Phillip Muller of Strategic Energy Limited (SEL)—a man who'd been a PG&E executive for 13 years. In an interview with the *Guardian*, Muller claimed that his experience with PG&E would be helpful because, he said, "I know PG&E and I know the people and I know the institution, so I can ask the right questions and get the information." Joel Ventresca of San Franciscans for Public Power saw it differently, suggesting dryly, "He's got PG&E's fingerprints all over him."

I immediately called for a special meeting of the select committee on municipal public power to investigate possible conflicts of interest in awarding the contract. I also asked for the test results, which would show how each consultant had scored. The fight for municipal power had been going on for 70 years, and some people in the city, like Bruce Brugmann at the *Guardian*, had been fighting for decades just for the opportunity to have a feasibility study conducted; I wasn't about to see PG&E and its lackeys win yet another victory by controlling the results in advance.

Before the select committee, it came out that Muller had received a substantial bonus as well as a future pension from PG&E when he left the company. Moreover, though SEL had scored highest, another potential conflict was apparent. The test results had clearly been tampered with. Under the "experience" category, one of the four PUC members scoring the bidders gave a zero to the second-place company, Economic and Technical Analysis Group (ETAG), effectively lowering its overall score. Yet ETAG had experience conducting other feasibility studies—though, admittedly, none of this specific type. In questioning the PUC members, both Supervisor Sue Bierman and I were unsatisfied with the answers we received. Larry Klein, the Hetch Hetchy executive director, refused to identify the member who gave ETAG the zero score.

I followed this up by introducing a pair of resolutions at the board to demand revocation of the contract and to force the PUC to identify the names of the raters on each evaluation scoring sheet.

I was also angered that the original bid guidelines seemed biased against public power. For example, the city's request for proposals failed even to include a demand that bidders study the Hetch Hetchy power system and the Raker Act public power mandate.

I authored a policy resolution urging the mayor to demand that the PUC immediately terminate the contract with SEL and review and reevaluate the contractor selection process. The resolution was approved by the board and, this time, signed by Mayor Jordan. A review committee was established, composed of both proponents and opponents of public power. Finally, on May 6, 1996, the review committee recommended hiring J. W. Wilson & Associates, which scored on the revised evaluation 133 points ahead of ETAG, the next closest bidder.

But the story didn't end there. I was informed that on the PUC's upcoming meeting agenda was an item calling for the award of the contract to one of the bidders. Although Wilson & Associates had already been recommended by the review committee, the PUC decided to choose ETAG, and we were back where we had been six months before. Though I'd been angered at the earlier selection of SEL the previous fall, I was now more incensed by the PUC's selection of ETAG over the review committee's recommended choice —Wilson & Associates.

I went back to the board with another piece of legislation, calling for the mayor to urge the PUC not to sign the ETAG contract because of conflict of interest and—as we'll soon see—its ties to PG&E. The legislation went into effect without the signature of the mayor. Subsequently, Mayor Brown did nothing to implement it.

I wasn't just being a picky consumer, always looking for a better choice. Not only had the PUC ignored the review committee's clear choice of Wilson & Associates, but the irregularities in this new selection process had gone too far. First, Larry Klein and Anson Moran, the PUC manager, had refused to disqualify ETAG even after the consultant belatedly disclosed that it had done at least

$140,000 worth of work for PG&E in the past. Second, the PUC never obtained a deposition that ETAG's project manager had given on behalf of PG&E in 1988 and that proved ETAG's bias toward PG&E and its opposition to public power. Third, the PUC did not require that ETAG provide examples of completed municipalization feasibility studies, a minimum standard required for any qualified bidder. Fourth, none of the examples that ETAG gave of its studies, including a confidential report, were public power feasibility studies or in any way comparable to the proposed San Francisco study. Fifth, Larry Klein gave the PUC an information packet containing a trade journal article critical of Wilson & Associates, but provided no other details of the review committee's discussions. Sixth, the protest that was filed by Wilson & Associates was reviewed by the PUC only in closed sessions. And finally, Larry Klein refused to disclose why the PUC rejected the protest by Wilson & Associates, claiming that the PUC's rejection was decided in secret meetings and he could not disclose what the PUC commissioners had discussed.

Even with all the testimony, I still had no verifiable proof that ETAG had been selected over Wilson & Associates for shady reasons. But Joel Ventresca pointed out that "this illogical decision smacks of backroom politicking; in my 25 years of activism in San Francisco I've never seen such an arrogant abuse of power by a city commission."

By now it had become apparent that the only choice left for me was to attempt to take away from the PUC the $150,000 the board had allocated them for the study. I asked the deputy city attorney for advice on this. He told me that since the PUC's decision had not yet been finalized, under the city's new charter I could draft a resolution setting up a procedure to select another consultant.

Throughout the long ordeal of trying to select a consultant, it had become obvious that to win, all the anti–public power faction had to do was to keep stalling. Term limits meant that I'd be long gone before any feasibility study was ever completed, or even before they selected a consultant. With the new rubber-stamp board of supervisors, and with the mayor's office firmly in PG&E's pocket (as most other mayors have been since 1927), the likelihood of public power, with its multimillion-dollar windfall for the city, remains only a distant hope.

Although several battles were won, over the years PG&E has been able to control the war over public power every step of the way. It has used the city's own paid staff to try to block every effort to stop the powerful utility monopoly from continuing to steal from San Francisco residents. In all of these hearings, PG&E has never had to send a representative or mount its own defense. In the war over public power, PG&E has been able to use the city's own PUC, Hetch Hetchy Project Manager Larry Klein, and even PUC Manager Anson Moran as its private lackeys. And in many instances over the past few years, it has also successfully used the mayor's office and members of the board of supervisors.

An armored-truck robbery, bad guys' guns blazing, might be of more visceral interest to the media. But in scope, it would pale in comparison.

One of the costs of not having public power in San Francisco is having to put up with PG&E's continual deceit over the franchise fee that it is required to pay the city to deliver consumer power over public property. The fee was set in 1939 at .5% of gross electricity sales. In reviewing similar fees in other cities, we found that the average electricity franchise fee is 4%—eight times what San Francisco has been getting for nearly 60 years.

In 1994 I wrote a piece of legislation that would have raised the electricity franchise fee rate to 2% in 1995 and to the national average of 4% between 1996 and 1999. The budget analyst estimated that an increase to 2% would generate annual revenues of $8.5 million, and the increase to 4% would generate $21 million. My strongest ally on this, as usual, was Supervisor Terence Hallinan.

The lobbying against this legislation was awesome. Nevertheless, no opposing argument made any sense. The board passed it and Mayor Jordan signed it.

After it was signed, PG&E claimed that the new regulation was illegal because the original 1939 agreement supposedly contained an "in-perpetuity" clause. We went downstairs to the city's dusty contract vault to look for the suddenly revealed clause. Not surprisingly, there was no such clause in the contract.

The select committee then discovered that PG&E had been supplying the Presidio military base with power since 1939 without ever having paid the city a franchise fee. This period included World War II, and the Korean and Vietnam Wars—periods when the Presidio was operating at its full military potential and using vast quantities of electricity. We checked the records and discovered that the city knew of this violation as early as 1941. The city attorney at that time had even ruled PG&E's actions illegal. Yet no money had ever been paid to the city for these 50 years. Nor had the city ever actively attempted to collect.

PG&E prodded their well-oiled litigation machinery into action. They moved to sue the city to block our attempt to collect the millions of dollars in unpaid franchise fees. Figuring they might as well kill two birds with one trip to the courthouse, they also sued to prevent any further efforts on our part to raise fees. Seeing no other choice, the select committee and the board instructed the city attorney's office to sue PG&E for failing to pay the city money it has been owed for more than half a century and for trespassing on public property.

PG&E knew what the public power advocates were up to. If we could establish a public power beachhead at the Presidio, we might be able eventually to achieve public power for the entire city. With the ownership of the Presidio shifting to the National Park Service, we wanted to provide the city with an opportunity to bid on supplying power. Meanwhile the Park Service had paid PG&E $80,000 to study the Presidio's electrical system, and PG&E had announced that upgrading the system would cost almost $23 million. PG&E told the Park Service that for that amount, they would gladly take the Presidio's electrical system off their hands—which they did. That's when we jumped into the picture, alleging that PG&E had an impermissible conflict of interest and that a competitive bidding process should be followed.

The Park Service decided to accept bids. Four groups entered the fray: the city, PG&E, a group called Women's Energy, and San Franciscans for Public Power. Faced with competition, PG&E informed the Park Service that it could upgrade the Presidio's power system at no cost to the Park Service—and returned the original $23 million. As in the Motorola case, this stresses the importance of a competitive bidding process. Competitive bidding always keeps quality and efficiency high and price low.

Guess who won the contract? When San Francisco lost the bid, the city protested and filed a lawsuit. All bidders who were not selected administratively filed protests.

In 1995, the U.S. Controller's Office ruled against both the city's appeal and the one filed by Women's Energy and San Franciscans for Public Power. The city immediately filed suit in federal court to appeal the decision because, in its request for proposals, the Park Service specifically required the bidder to have a franchise license to deliver gas and electricity to the Presidio. We contended that PG&E had never had such a license and had not paid the franchise fee in 55 years. We also contended that federal competitive bidding forbids agencies such as the Park Service from awarding contracts to anyone performing systems engineering work or providing technical direction for the system, as PG&E had done.

We're still waiting.

Opponents of public power claim that the city doesn't have the expertise to manage a municipal power system in San Francisco. For nearly 70 years, PG&E and its lobbyists have successfully convinced voters that the city is unreliable and that if it can't even fix potholes, it certainly can't manage power. But PG&E service has continued to decline at the same time that its rates to consumers are among the highest in the nation. What people don't know is that the city has been providing its own power, with very few maintenance problems, to 1,370 city buildings, our public transportation system, the Port of San Francisco, and the airport for decades, saving millions of dollars for local taxpayers and benefiting the general fund every year. The general fund is like the private bank account of the citizens of a city—it is an important source of local funding.

Opponents also don't realize that cities from Los Angeles to Sacramento have municipal power. Why have these facts been kept secret when the whole city could be on public power for less cost to the consumer and more money to the general fund? The answer, please: PG&E, which has made hundreds of millions of dollars on the existing arrangement, and local politicians who have been either too crooked or too fearful or too lazy to fight this giant monopoly.

This information is not mere campaign rhetoric. If I based a political campaign on PG&E material, voters would fall asleep. PG&E has made sure that few people care. But the simple fact of the matter is that PG&E owes a great deal of money to San Francisco, and they should no longer be permitted to continue merrily along with not paying what they owe the city, and therefore the people, of San Francisco.

This is about more than some cranky people in California demanding changes to an obscure system. It's a blistering example of how government is no longer owned by its citizens—if it ever was.

In January 1996, when I was running against John Burton for the California State Senate, I was informed by Stan Smith of the San Francisco Labor Council that I would not be considered for the council's endorsement. As it turned out, there was a little-known resolution prohibiting the council from considering any candidate who supported public power. I was informed of this only three days prior to the endorsement meeting, so I had little chance to gather support. I was told that I might as well not even show up at the meeting.

So PG&E, along with the political machine, was setting in motion the mechanism to keep me from office.

One of the key member groups in the San Francisco Labor Council is the International Brotherhood of Electrical Workers (IBEW), the union representing PG&E employees. Stan Smith's wife is Kathy Maas, business manager of the IBEW. PG&E had convinced the union that public power was not in their best interest. Maas reported that her union was against public power because, as she said, "I don't believe that the city and county of San Francisco could or would be as good an employer as PG&E."

I've been an advocate for public power my entire elected life, but I've also been a strong union supporter at the same time. My father was a staunchly pro-union mayor, and I believe in the rights of the working men and women; but union members aren't always told what the union leadership is up to.

I showed up at the endorsement meeting anyway, and was told that I couldn't speak because of the rules against endorsing anyone who advocates public power—even though the IBEW had already endorsed me. I'd been endorsed by both labor and the electrical union specifically for eight years, and now, suddenly, this rule was being imposed. Running against Willie Brown had been bad, but it was nothing compared to running against PG&E.

The council finally let me speak. I explained how public power could save millions of dollars, which could be channeled into better worker benefits. I pointed out PG&E's history of corporate downsizing and its firing of 3,000 employees two years before, none of whom had received severance pay or health benefits. I drew attention to labor's endorsement that evening for Supervisors Carole Migden and Kevin Shelley, both of whom had supported public power. Somehow the pro–public-power voting record of these candidates didn't get in their way. But then, neither of them had fought as hard as I had for public power. Neither of them had created and chaired the select committee on municipal public power. Neither of them had taken on PG&E over the issue of the franchise fees. And neither of them had gone up against the PUC to ensure the independence of a feasibility study for public power.

Maybe I should have taken heed of Dick Clarke's warning to Art Agnos about playing ball.

That night it became obvious to me that PG&E and the Burton–Brown machine were in bed together. PG&E had just donated over $100,000 for Willie Brown's mayoral inauguration party. Brown later named Dick Clarke the head of his spring 1996 economic summit.

The fires keep burning.

The Presidio of San Francisco is a historic former army base on San Francisco Bay. Maybe you saw the movie *The Presidio* with Sean Connery. It is also a large chunk of desirable real estate in the most expensive neighborhood in the most expensive city in America. To call Presidio land "valuable" is like calling Mount Everest "tall." It's incomprehensibly valuable. It sits on high land overlooking the water and the Marin Headlands. The Golden Gate Bridge juts out from the front of it. It's surrounded by multimillion-dollar houses. It's covered with trees and park space. Roads and buildings are already built.

In 1996, the U.S. Senate passed historic parks legislation that turned 80% of the Presidio's 1,480 acres over to a nonprofit government trust that will have broad powers to manage and lease the Presidio's historic buildings. The legislation takes the Presidio away from the National Park Service and places it into the hands of the private Presidio Trust, a semi-independent entity with "expertise in finance, planning, real estate and resource conservation." The reality of this situation, and how it came to pass, is another shining example of the real motivation behind political action.

In 1972, when Phil Burton secured passage of legislation creating the Golden Gate National Recreation Area, he got Congress to agree to transfer the Presidio to the National Park Service if and when the U.S. Army moved out. When this finally occured, plans began floating around to transform the Presidio's buildings into a university, an environmental center, or something like a West Coast United Nations, while Republicans talked of selling off the property for development, raising billions of dollars for the national debt.

Everyone wanted the Presidio. The city wanted to turn it into a national park. Environmentalists wanted to restore it. And commercial developers wanted a piece of the multibillion-dollar potential sitting up there, looking out over the bay.

Although there had been discussion of open public debate on the Presidio's future, sharp budget cuts had left the National Park Service unable to pay for even basic planning studies. There was no way they could pick up the cost of converting, maintaining, and managing the largest urban national park in the nation, especially when many of the 510 buildings were in need of serious repair.

So in 1991 the National Park Service asked the Golden Gate National Park Association to help raise money to plan for the conversion. Together they created the Presidio Council, composed of some two dozen members, mostly from business—this was not an objective group of players. Many had close ties to downtown business and development interests. In fact, the head of the Golden Gate National Park Association, Tony Rosenblatt, was a wealthy pro-development investor and the former head of the San Francisco Planning Commission. Also on the Presidio Council was our old friend Dick Clarke, PG&E's chief executive officer. At one time, PG&E had three of its corporate directors on the Presidio Council. Others included the founder of The Gap, which, by 1994, had made it known that it wanted to lease up to a million square feet at the Presidio's main post to establish a shopping center for environmentally conscious businesses.

During the Presidio planning process a lot of groups jockeyed for position. The reason for the involvement of business interests was obvious: they smelled money, low-cost and tax-free office space, upscale malls, and the potential to develop and then sell high-end housing in a city short of vacant land. Only a naïve fool would be surprised that moneyed interests were sniffing around.

It was the environmentalists' involvement that shocked me. Instead of fighting for its environmental protection and low-density use, some, like Michael Alexander, chair of the Sierra Club Presidio Task Force, supported limited development while the Sierra Club as a whole considered moving into office space in the Presidio—not what you'd expect from an organization committed to the environment, but perhaps in line with a group that wanted a prestigious new address. The Sierra Club and other groups went along for the ride with the Presidio Council. Although Michael Alexander later denied it, he applied to be a tenant.

In the process, individuals like Alexander advanced their own prestige by rubbing elbows with senators, members of Congress, and local big-business interests. When I went to the Sierra Club's endorsement-committee interview during the 1995 mayor's race, I asked them, "How can you guys promote something that would create a mini-downtown high-rise mall complex?" The committee had no response, didn't discuss it and claimed that Alexander wasn't representing their interests. But the Sierra Club name and those of other groups were being used by the Presidio Council to promote the trust to the public. And it worked.

The final plans prepared by the Park Service, with money and help from the Presidio Council, were vague. They included lofty-sounding general goals like "preserving and enhancing cultural and natural resources" and creating new programs through public/private partnerships. They also called for the creation of a Presidio corporation, a trust that would oversee all decisions, including those related to new development. Working with the Presidio Council, Representative Nancy Pelosi introduced H.R. 3433, which would have taken the "built environment" away from the Park Service and given it to the private Presidio Trust. Members of the trust would have been appointed by the president of the United States from a short list, over which Pelosi undoubtedly has some input. Given those historically involved, the names seemed likely to include several of those who'd already been involved in the Presidio Council —the major business interests of San Francisco.

It was a moot point. The bill was tossed into the fire. The U.S. Senate killed it in 1994.

The following March, Pelosi introduced a new bill, H.R. 1296. She had amended the title of the original bill, "To Provide for the Administration of Certain Presidio Properties," by adding the phrase "at Minimal Expense to the Federal Taxpayer." As this new bill was moving through Representative James Hansen's (R-Utah) subcommittee, a few local groups in San Francisco, notably the Marina Civic Improvement and Property Owners Association, came out against it, calling it a bad management model. This group wanted to preserve the important architecture and open, parklike feel of the Presidio and to keep the density low. They were afraid that the trust would rehabilitate every shed, rent them all out to tenants, and increase the overall density of use. By the time Pelosi's bill somehow got through Hansen's subcommittee, however, it had been altered to allow the trust to replace lower-priority historic buildings with new construction. Their only restriction was maximum square footage—developers couldn't go above the preexisting maximum of six million square feet.

In April 1995, several of us got wind of a private meeting that Pelosi was holding locally on the Presidio. This meeting was never publicly announced, even though Representative Hansen was scheduled to be there, along with Representative Ralph Regula, the House Interior Appropriations subcommittee chair. At this meeting the activists were barred from the room. Although Hansen agreed to a local hearing, Pelosi said she didn't think it was possible. Shockingly, even the newly-appointed executive director of San Francisco Planning and Urban Research advised against a public hearing.

The promoters of the bill may have feared that a public hearing would bring out opposition to the plan and prevent passage of the bill. But by closing off discussion, they took the future of the Presidio out of the hands of San Francisco residents and placed it into the hands of seven politically appointed private citizens. Current legislation now calls for these appointments to be made by the president of the United States.

It's apparent that big-money people have already been picked. These are not Republicans or Democrats, but San Francisco's moneyed interests. The legislation calls for these appointees to have "expertise in finance, planning, real estate and resource conservation." In addition, there's a whole bureaucracy being built into the trust, one that allows the appointees to hire staff and set salaries with complete flexibility. (At the time of this writing, the *San Francisco Chronicle* had just reported that Mayor Willie Brown had told President Clinton that he wanted to be one of the appointees—and Nancy Pelosi had concurred.)

Our elected leaders are clearly returning some big favors.

The trust will be given control to make all decisions without any public oversight. There will be only two public hearings a year, and the city of San Francisco will have little to no input. Moreover, though appointees to the trust can serve up to only eight years, they can sign 55- and 99-year leases on Presidio sites, thus setting the rules for the next century.

They can also sign these leases without mandatory competitive bidding. The law's wording states that they should obtain "reasonable competition." But this is a giant loophole. Can you imagine being on the Presidio Trust and having your friend say to you, "I'll take the whole Letterman Hospital complex"? How are you going to determine fair market value? In addition, there's nothing to prevent the new tenant from subleasing it at a higher rate to someone else and pocketing the difference.

The legislation no longer includes the "conflict-of-interest" clause that was written into the original bill. The old bill had stated that "no member of the Presidio Trust shall have a financial interest in any tenant or have development interest in any tenant." That entire clause has been removed. The explanation for this from congressional staff is that the Ethics in Government Act applies to the trust board.

I'm sure.

The legislation also allows for trading square footage, demolishing old structures, and constructing new buildings, all without input from the city. Take the Letterman Hospital complex as an example. The University of California might want a part, and companies like Genentech might be interested. Or the entire building could be replaced with a shopping mall.

Worse yet, while the maximum-square-footage restriction sounds good, the loophole for new construction could allow for the replacement of the military housing above Baker Beach, facing the Pacific Ocean, with newly constructed high-end homes—each with a 99-year lease. This is done in Orange County, in Southern California, all the time. The developer holds the 99-year lease, while people buy and sell the houses. This possibility has been confirmed by the Presidio's general manager.

There's six million square feet of built space at the Presidio. Therefore, the trust appointees or their friends can make money three different ways: by becoming master tenants and subleasing properties at higher rates, by developing the military housing site, and by administering the existing officers' housing formerly occupied by command-rank officers. Many of these homes are historic, but others are not. A lot of them could easily be demolished and rebuilt.

The trust legislation also gives the trust the right to borrow from a $50 million revolving fund from the federal treasury. These guaranteed loans can be used for new construction and rehabilitation. Without any form of public oversight, there's nothing to prevent the Presidio from being stripped of its historic resources and parklike ambiance and developed with low-interest federal loans as a business park and shopping complex, all at a profit to individual business interests. After being stripped, the Presidio could then be given back to the government with taxpayers responsible for repayment but with all the leases in place for decades to come.

Finally, the trust will be competing with downtown San Francisco for office space but will have an advantage since the Presidio is considered a tax-free zone. This means that businesses can move from downtown to the Presidio's "prestige address" and reduce their expenditures by being exempt from gross-receipts or payroll taxes. This will in turn represent a drop in city revenues.

When I was a child, until I married and left home, I grew up in a house that overlooked the Presidio. As a family, we took walks through the woods and enjoyed it as a part of our city's and nation's heritage. It had been there since the Spanish established a fort in the late 1700s, and was later taken over by Mexico and then the U.S. Army. The gift of the Presidio to the National Park Service was a gift to America, and especially a gift to the residents of San Francisco. It is a gem to be preserved, not developed.

But the thieves who are turning the Presidio into a cash mill have different ideas. They have the power to bring about legislation that will rob not only money—though plenty of that—but also a historical treasure from American citizens.

The cases of PG&E and Motorola exemplify the power of corporations to sway our elected leaders into passing laws favorable to the corporate world in general and individual corporations specifically. But perhaps even more insidious and personally self-serving—corporations and politics are made up of individual people who are interested in increasing their own wealth, after all—is the case of the Presidio Trust, in which a variety of business interests and politicians have fought to secure absolute control to manage and develop the jewel in San Francisco's crown and the most valuable piece of open urban space in America. This case shows how private interests and politicians routinely come together around a mixture of subtle half-bribes and the fear of worst-case scenarios to achieve their goals. Whether the leverage is token power, cash, the promise of local jobs, or threats to cut old-growth redwood forests, corporate interests have successfully chosen from the same set of strategies to get what they want in nearly every community nationwide.

What makes these particular acts so intolerable is the involvement of public officials in these thefts, the lack of real opposition and opportunities for public debate, and the real or potential costs to the public. At the same time that critical health, social, and community services continue to be cut, those in power have been unwilling to stand up to corporate interests in ways that could bring in vast revenues, reduce expenditures for taxpayers, and save costs to consumers. If the local cases that I've discussed here are any example, the amount of corruption at the state and national levels must be enormous.

All of these cases are similar to others that have gone on elsewhere, yesterday and today. This kind of corporate and political greed was present in the land grants to railroads in opening the West, and it's still present today. The shadow of lobbyists, corrupt politicians, and rapacious corporations and private interests can be seen everywhere, whether we're talking about federal contracts for defense or other services, or giveaways of land rights to ranching, mining, logging, or oil interests. In all of these cases, the public suffers. Corporations and their elected puppets may promise increased jobs, lower costs, or better service, but the end result of many of these endeavors has often been increased costs to taxpayers and consumers, destruction of the environment, increased corporate profits, re-elections for corporate-sponsored politicians, and massive profits to the individuals and groups that pull the strings.

This is what's being robbed: our right to a government of the people.

This is who's doing it: corporate interests and their political puppets.

This is why they're getting away with it: *we're letting them.*

TRAITORS TO COUNTRY:
THE TOBACCO INDUSTRY

"Now," said I, "be dumb,
Accursed traitor! To thy shame, of thee
True tidings will I bear."

INFERNO, CANTO XXXII

T HE LOWEST LEVELS OF HELL ARE COLD. The section of the frozen pit to which traitors to their country are sent is called Antenora, named after the man who Dante believed betrayed Troy to the Greeks. The damned of this pit are trapped from the neck down in a frozen lake. Dante, who begins his journey through Hell showing some degree of sympathy for the damned, kicks these spirits in their heads as he passes. They have sold out their homeland for money.

Can we really point this condemning a finger at the tobacco industry? Though a favorite whipping boy in the press and among activists, surely the industry is just trying to make a buck in a free-market economy, as it has every right to do. How can we say that they are selling out their country?

Like this: America's children are being seduced toward a premature death of cancer. Our future generations are in the hands of corporations whose sole purpose is to sell cigarettes, and cigarettes are devices which *by design* deliver carcinogens into the human body.

The politicians who either stand silent or play ball with tobacco corporations are selling out the American people for their own personal gain.

People who ignore or deny the whole thing are complicit.

One major cause of America's current health care crisis has been the indefensible actions of the tobacco industry and the politicians who have willingly served them over the years by blocking antismoking legislation. While apparent paybacks and the unethical use of political power are seen daily in cases like those of Motorola and

PG&E, the economic and social effects of such behavior are nothing compared to the devastating offspring of the marriage of tobacco and politics. Together, the tobacco industry and their elected yes-men have acted as merchants of death to countless numbers of people over the past several decades. Not even taking into account the tens of millions of dollars the government has paid over the years to subsidize the growing of tobacco, the human and financial costs of this relationship have amounted to millions of deaths and billions of dollars in medical costs to taxpayers and consumers.

Cigarettes kill more people each year than all homicides, suicides, automobile accidents, accidents at work and home, fires, and deaths from AIDS, heroin, cocaine, and alcohol *combined*. Estimates place the annual number of deaths from tobacco-related illnesses at three million worldwide and more than half a million Americans, with annual public and private medical costs of smoking-related illnesses amounting to tens of billions of dollars in this country alone.

Unlike many other health-related issues, however, the problem of tobacco in this country is one that we may eventually solve, as it lends itself to a number of solutions. And the victories against the tobacco industry that have begun and, I believe, will continue, give us hope that we can also solve the other problems we face.

While many politicians have enthusiastically touted wars against drugs and violence, and have repeatedly called for harsher sentences for multiple offenders and drug dealers, many of these same politicians have looked the other way for years and enabled the deadly proliferation of the tobacco drug. Moreover, they have continued to take tobacco industry money to do their bidding, often blocking antismoking legislation.

Like many people, I used to assume that smoking was an act of choice. And like many, I used to smoke. Although I knew that it might be bad for my health, it was a roll of the dice and a choice for which I felt I was ultimately responsible. The tobacco industry was merely providing smokers with a product that was part of the history and culture of America. Like other activities, if smoking was potentially dangerous to my health, it was up to me to do something about it.

I quit in August 1988 because my children convinced me to. (They also were constantly hiding my cigarettes.) But I also felt a sense of outrage and intense anger toward the tobacco industry. I'd read some secret tobacco industry memos that had been made public, describing how companies had deliberately targeted their sales campaigns to children and women of certain ethnic groups. With three million customers dying each year, it's crucial for the industry to find ready replacements. And the industry believed that children—the most vulnerable population—were the best source. Studies have shown that 90% of smokers begin before they're 19 years old. If you don't begin smoking as a teenager, chances are you never will. Knowing this, the tobacco industry deliberately targeted this group. They also realized that women and ethnic populations were similarly vulnerable.

Although I was criticized for it, I believed that, as a local government, we could take on the tobacco industry. I felt that we didn't have to wait for the federal government and state legislatures to do something first.

In 1989, my first year as a San Francisco supervisor, I began work on the first of my antismoking measures. The maliciousness of the industry's actions and their obvious lies and continuous denials about the hazards of smoking had convinced me that something needed to be done locally. After all, it was at the local level where nonsmokers—both adults and children—were faced with the hazards of secondhand smoke. After all, all politics is local.

In 1990 I introduced legislation to ban smoking in restaurants. The existing city law, passed in 1984, set aside only minimal nonsmoking areas, which were often composed of a few tables here and there. These smoking and nonsmoking areas were not really separate—nonsmokers were not really being protected, and smoke was free to circulate. The law needed serious tightening. The only compromise I was willing to make was in the case of restaurants with bars. My proposed legislation allowed smoking in bars, but banned it in restaurants themselves. I would have preferred banning smoking in bars as well, but there was no chance of an ordinance passing with such a provision at that time.

There are over 4,000 restaurants in San Francisco. Since the majority of them don't have bars, most would have been affected. I received serious opposition from both the restaurant lobby—the Golden Gate Restaurant Association (GGRA)—and the tobacco industry. The GGRA was afraid this law would drive smoking customers from restaurants. The tobacco lobby, of course, saw it as a dangerous precedent. My legislation was labeled both radical and reactionary. I was called a "puritan," a "fascist," and a "nazi." Opponents claimed I was restricting smokers' rights. The real message —that I was trying to protect the health of nonsmokers—wasn't getting out. My proposed legislation failed by a six-to-five vote of the San Francisco Board of Supervisors.

Although the first round was a tough loss, I wasn't about to give up. I realized that if I was going to succeed, I'd need to start slowly and defuse opposition from the GGRA. As simple a strategy as it sounds, I began presenting plaques and certificates of honor to restaurants that voluntarily prohibited smoking, and I also began meeting with restaurant owners to explain the benefits of such legislation. This worked, and gradually I began to chip away at the tobacco lobby without their awareness of what I was really doing. I introduced smaller pieces of antitobacco legislation that didn't cause the same uproar, and the lobby eased up on their opposition. This was their mistake, as I was only waiting for the climate to change before I tried again.

In 1991 I authored an ordinance outlawing cigarette vending machines in San Francisco, except in locations to which minors had no access. Who could argue against this proposal? Studies show that children are major users of vending machines, and access to most machines can't be controlled. The ordinance passed and was signed into law by the mayor. I'd gotten my foot in the door.

The next year I decided to fight tobacco advertising on city property. In my view, the real harm in advertising was to teenagers and children, and the majority of advertising was being conducted at the local level. Although the industry disputes it, advertising has never been designed to get people to switch brands; it's designed to get children to start. For example, in a study by various authors, including University of California at San Francisco researcher Stanley Glantz, researchers proved that if brand switching *was* the goal of advertising, it was a poor use of money. Glantz and his colleagues found that companies spent the equivalent of $345 each year in advertising for each person who actually switched brands, grossing only $347 per year from these customers, or $2 in gross revenues per person. Clearly, the industry had another purpose.

It was obvious to me that advertising was crucial to the industry because of a simple thing called mortality. Over a thousand people a day in this country die from tobacco-related illnesses, and others quit. Not only do older populations continue to die off, but smokers die off faster than the rest of the populace. To keep their profits up, the industry has to replace consumers. Where do they go to find them? According to interoffice memos made public by whistleblowers, the "hooking period" is from 8 to 14 years of age.

Advertising has maliciously targeted adolescents. Tobacco industry memos point out that boys are especially nervous during puberty, and girls suffer more at this time from low self-esteem. Philip Morris for years has used images of the independent cowboy to increase sales of Marlboros to youth who crave their own independence. But the industry crossed a line in the 1980s. Richard Kluger points out in his book *Ashes to Ashes* that R.J. Reynolds created the cartoon figure Joe Camel—the "smooth character" and "party animal"—to sell Camel cigarettes, which previously had appealed to a mostly older, blue-collar, rural smoker. Now, of course, Joe Camel is everywhere, and youthful, hip T-shirts, posters, and other Joe Camel paraphernalia can be purchased with "C-notes" found in Camel packs.

COURTESY OF PHIL FRANK

210

The impact of the Joe Camel ad campaign was made evident in a study published in 1991 in the *Journal of the American Medical Association*. This study found that 30% of three-year-olds and 90% of six-year-olds knew that the Joe Camel image was connected with cigarettes. This brand-name recall rate was higher even than that of Mickey Mouse. Further, this figure was near total for those in high school, with 98% identifying the link, compared with only 67% of adults. Obviously, youth were being targeted. Unfortunately, while Joe Camel won't die of lung cancer, our young people will.

Although I initially wanted a total advertising ban, I realized that the only way my legislation would pass would be by grandfathering in existing contracts, and then dealing with those separately. As a result, I authored both an ordinance prohibiting tobacco product advertising on most city-owned properties and a policy resolution urging all city boards, commissions, and departments to request individuals and entities with current advertising rights to stop advertising cigarettes and tobacco products and to renegotiate leases, permits, and agreements to ban all such advertising. Again there was opposition, but evidence of the link between advertising and teen smoking was undeniable. As a result, my ordinance and policy resolution both passed and were signed into law by the mayor.

At that point the city had a number of existing contracts with advertising subcontractors. After we passed the policy resolution, some of these were grandfathered in; others bowed out. Our subcontractors included Gannett Outdoor, with its contract for bus shelters throughout the city; George Broder, representing the Patrick Media Company with its billboards; and JCDecaux, the French company that maintains the large kiosks and public toilets throughout downtown. Now, remember that tobacco companies are the largest paying advertisers in the world. They spend massive amounts of money on advertising, more than $5 billion each year in this country alone. Yet we were ultimately successful. When we asked Lou Lillian at Gannett to stop tobacco advertising on our bus shelters and near schools, he agreed voluntarily. Imagine a large advertising company, making piles of money from tobacco ads, agreeing to tell their clients "No more advertising."

This was an overwhelming victory.

Beginning in late 1992, three events occurred that encouraged me to step up my fight against the tobacco industry. The first was the November election, which gave me the board presidency and the increased power that this entailed. Second was the growing public outrage over the obvious lies and deceit being perpetrated by the industry. Tobacco shot itself in the foot—or maybe even in the head—when those industry executives stood before Representative Henry Waxman's congressional panel, right hands raised, and denied the health risks of tobacco and the addictive power of nicotine in the face of over 6,000 studies to the contrary. The third event was the release of the Environmental Protection Agency (EPA) report on secondhand smoke and the agency's classification of it as a class A-1 carcinogen. Their fact sheet points out that thousands of non-smoking adults die each year as a result of secondhand smoke. They also found it to be a contributing factor each year in a million cases of childhood asthma and 300,000 cases of pneumonia and bronchitis in infants as old as 18 months, 15,000 of whom require hospitalization.

I never thought reading the words *class A-1 carcinogen* would make me feel like celebrating, but this was the smoking gun, as it were, that I needed. In early 1993 I reintroduced my original legislation banning smoking in all restaurants in San Francisco—with workplaces and sports arenas added. The *San Francisco Examiner* endorsed it two weeks later. By now, I'd won some support from the GGRA; after the EPA report, there was no way they'd fight any ordinance regulating smoking in restaurants. After a pitched battle with the tobacco lobby, the new ordinance passed the board and was signed into law by the mayor. Although Frank Jordan was a conservative who normally would have opposed any measure that restricted business, his wife, Wendy Paskin, a fanatic about health, convinced him to sign it. He could have stolen away four of my votes but, thanks to Wendy, he didn't.

This ordinance, which became law in 1994, was not only the strongest antismoking measure in California at the time, it was also one of the strictest smoking bans in the nation. Since then, other cities have followed suit. The GGRA has discovered that their fears of losing revenue were unfounded; in fact, restaurant attendance has actually *increased* since the ban. Restaurants are far more pleasant places for everyone now, and customers are approving the ban with their wallets.

We'd breached the industry's barricades. In 1994, the Occupational Safety and Health Administration changed the federal regulations to prohibit smoking in the workplace. I immediately authored a policy resolution supporting these proposed changes. It passed and was signed by the mayor.

After the bans passed, Assemblyman Terry Friedman called me and said he was thinking of applying the legislation to a state bill. I was excited. I drove to Sacramento and met with him a couple of times. He introduced the bill to the assembly, and it passed in 1995, over the objections of then-Speaker Willie Brown. The issue was too big and too popular for Brown to defeat, even with his hundreds of thousands of tobacco industry dollars. California wanted the law.

Friedman's legislation prohibits public smoking a step at a time. In the first year, 1996, smoking was banned in workplaces and restaurants. Smoking in bars was to be banned in 1997, but the tobacco industry and their political lackeys have been trying to amend the law to push the final implementation back to the year 2000; they have already been successful in delaying by at least a year the 1997 implementation.

Next I went after Candlestick Park, which had been exempted from the advertising ban. I authored a policy resolution urging the removal of all tobacco advertising from the stadium. Though cigarettes couldn't be advertised on television, home broadcasts of Giants games showed a large Marlboro sign in the outfield, clearly visible to the home-plate camera. This clever tobacco industry ploy, repeated in stadiums and arenas around the country, is obviously a terrible message to send children watching the game on television. This resolution passed too.

As far as I'm concerned, anyone fighting this type of legislation is suspect; I'd assume they have the backing of the tobacco industry. From the day I started work on my antitobacco legislation, the industry was calling my brothers, attempting to solicit them as lawyers, and even calling and attempting to hire my friends, all in an effort to put personal pressure on me to stop. In one case they apparently hired a friend of mine who then asked me to cancel my planned committee hearing on tobacco. It was an odd request, since the two of us had never discussed politics, and she joked that she'd been hired by the industry. A Los Angeles lobbyist later confirmed this, telling me that she'd received $50,000. If this is true, it's an immoral outrage.

Even with our significant local victories, I believed that real change would have to come at the federal level and in the courtrooms. I felt it was necessary to put pressure on Washington whenever possible and support the federal government whenever it was heading in the right direction. I authored policy resolutions supporting the national petition drive to put tobacco products under the regulation of the Food and Drug Administration and plans by President Clinton and the FDA to reduce smoking by adolescents and children by regulating tobacco products. Both resolutions passed the board and were signed by the mayor.

In early 1996, the tobacco industry's favorite legislator, former Speaker of the assembly Willie Brown, became mayor of San Francisco. During his years as Speaker, this Napoleonic political master had taken more tobacco money than any other elected official in American history, receiving over three-quarters of a million dollars in campaign donations, gifts, honoraria, and legal fees from tobacco interests between 1984 and 1995. In exchange, Brown voted three times against Terry Friedman's bill for a smoke-free workplace. He was one of the leading opponents of that measure and lobbied hard against it. He also voted in favor of a ban on local cigarette taxes and, most blatant of all, coauthored a product liability bill that pointedly exempted tobacco from product liability lawsuits. The Willie L. Brown–Bill Lockyer Civil Liability Reform Act of 1987 has made it impossible for California residents who suffer from smoking-related illnesses to sue tobacco firms for damages.

In 1990, Brown traveled to Louisville at the expense of Philip Morris for the Kentucky Derby, and met with industry executives to discuss how to bypass local antismoking laws. The release of a memo documenting this in 1991 by the American Cancer Society caused an uproar in Sacramento, which fortunately led to the failure of an industry- and Brown-backed smoking control bill. The proposition, which was a statewide voter initiative in 1994, was disguised as a tough "antismoking" bill, but in reality it would have enacted lenient statewide smoking controls and superseded dozens of much stricter local antismoking ordinances.

Richard Kluger quotes Brown in *Ashes to Ashes*: "I'm not concerned about smoking—it's not my issue. I'm concerned about substance abuse." Apart from the fact that Brown represented a big-time drug dealer in the 1980s, he conveniently avoided the fact that tobacco is an addictive substance that is abused more widely than any other drug, and that tobacco companies are in the business of trafficking in these drugs. He also ignores the impact of tobacco-related illnesses on various ethnic groups, as well as the fact that African Americans have been targeted relentlessly by the industry and die at substantially higher rates from smoking-related diseases than other groups. African American lung cancer rates are 40% to 50% higher than that of any other group.

The lowest part of Dante's Hell, the pit of Satan, is a frozen lake. Satan is a three-headed beast trapped in the ice. The maws of the heads are chewing on the three worst traitors in history: Brutus and Cassius, who betrayed Caesar in a bid to seize the Roman Empire, and Judas, who sold Christ to the Romans for 30 pieces of silver.

How much money is enough to sell out the future of your people?

When Brown was elected mayor of San Francisco, it looked like the success of my antitobacco work would come to an end. But it didn't, and this illustrates the popularity of antismoking legislation. Thank God some issues like smoking are bigger than individual politicians, bigger than lobbyists, and bigger even than political machines. Issues can grow to this size when they have the support of the public, when the timing is right, and when there's a huge body of indisputable evidence behind them. This is what happened in the case of Willie Brown and tobacco.

During Brown's first nine months of office, I introduced ten pieces of antitobacco legislation, all of which passed the board. Brown signed all ten. He couldn't oppose such legislation, especially in San Francisco, a town that has been an American leader in anti-smoking campaigns. As mayor, Brown has had to largely abandon his pro-tobacco stance under the microscope of city politics, especially since the most damning piece of information used against him in the mayoral race was the amount of money he had accepted from the tobacco industry.

The first piece of legislation that we sent to his desk was a policy resolution supporting California Assembly Bill 2055, which allows local jurisdictions to establish a cigarette excise tax. The purpose of this bill was to liberate local governments from restrictions that Brown had authored or supported as Speaker.

Next, I introduced a policy resolution urging the San Francisco Retirement Board to divest securities holdings in publicly traded companies that derive revenue from the sale of tobacco products. It also urged the state legislature to pass legislation barring state and municipal pension funds from holding tobacco company stocks. As president of the board of supervisors in 1993 and 1994, I was one of five members of the retirement board, and we oversaw funds totaling $6.8 billion. I hoped we might be able to put economic pressure on the industry in the same way that many governments had in antiapartheid divestiture of South African companies. Beyond this, however, I believed that it was immoral to make money from supporting an industry that kills people.

Over the next few months I introduced several other resolutions: supporting H.R. 969, which banned smoking on all scheduled commercial airline flights; urging the FDA to require that all cigarette ingredients be listed on the package; urging the FDA to establish regulations requiring the rating of tar and nicotine levels in cigarettes; urging California Attorney General Dan Lungren to institute litigation against tobacco companies to recover the costs of caring for people with smoking-related illnesses; and opposing any proposed restrictions on, or any legislation that would restrict, Proposition 99 tobacco research and media programs. All of these passed and were signed, reluctantly, by the new mayor.

Most telling is another resolution that passed and was signed by Brown. This one urged the legislature to amend Section 1714.45 of the Willie L. Brown–Bill Lockyer Civil Liability Reform Act of 1987, which had granted immunity to tobacco manufacturers from consumer product liability lawsuits filed in California. Rumor had it that the act had been penned on a napkin in the Sacramento restaurant where Brown met with tobacco industry officials. Later, the

217

story goes, the actual legislation was drafted by tobacco industry lawyers. Section 1714.45 sold out the health of California citizens.

An amendment at the state level like the one we urged in San Francisco is necessary if California is ever going to join other states in filing a lawsuit against the tobacco industry to recover the costs for unreimbursed treatment of tobacco-related illnesses. What I want is to amend the law to drop just one exempted industry: tobacco. This was my intent in drafting the resolution. To take this one step further, however, I secured the support of independent State Senator Quentin Kopp, who agreed to introduce this legislation at the state level.

Like my antismoking city ordinance, Kopp's legislation will eventually pass. The time has come. There's no way that elected officials can afford to look like they're still in bed with tobacco companies, especially when so many other states have taken bold action against the industry.

To protect America's health, we have to fight the tobacco industry on several fronts. Preserving the health of nonsmokers is a must, and ordinances that ban smoking in restaurants, public settings, and workplaces is a good way to begin. If we can reduce the number of children who start smoking, we can ultimately reduce the number of tobacco-related illnesses and deaths. The best way to accomplish this is by controlling advertising and access to cigarettes.

Although San Francisco is a small city, our health budget incurs tens of millions of dollars each year in unreimbursed expenses from tobacco-related illnesses. This money could go to combating homelessness and increasing services to children, the mentally ill, and those with AIDS; to keeping crisis clinics open; or to hiring more police. Instead, like other cities and states, we pay hospital bills while the tobacco industry grimly reaps its vast profits. But unlike other cities and states, we have to contend with the Brown-Lockyer Act.

I decided to follow the course that had been set by a number of states in suing the tobacco industry. The lawsuit would have been more damaging to the industry if Attorney General Dan Lungren had brought the suit, but because of the Brown–Lockyer Act—and because Governor Pete Wilson has been a supporter of tobacco interests—the state is barred from initiating its own lawsuit against the industry. Quentin Kopp's legislation to amend the California Civil Code might take months.

I decided San Francisco would sue tobacco on its own.

Section 1714.45, however, also prevents cities from suing the tobacco industry for product liability. To get around this problem, I studied the lawsuit filed by Texas, and I came up with a cause of action—San Francisco should not sue as a consumer for product liability; we should sue as the *employer* of a consumer. As an employer, San Francisco has been obliged to pay the costs for smoking-related illnesses suffered by that consumer. We're also suing for fraud and violations of the Racketeer Influenced and Corrupt Organizations (RICO) Act. And because of Section 1714.45, the city has to file the lawsuit in federal court.

To initiate this process, I wrote Resolution 46996, instructing the city attorney to sue the tobacco industry and outlining explicitly how she should implement the lawsuit. To get that far, however, I had to bring it before the health committee, hold public hearings on it, and then bring it to the full board for a vote. This took about four months, and by the time we were ready for a final vote, I had been able to get eight of my board colleagues to agree to co-sponsor it—enough to override a mayoral veto. If everything went according to plan, I'd get the full support of the board, and Brown would have to sign it, probably gritting his teeth as he did.

Five minutes before the vote, in walked City Attorney Louise Renne and the head of the city health department, Sandra

Hernandez. The city attorney demanded an immediate closed-door private session of the board. She wanted a confidential attorney-client–privilege meeting, where no one could sit in, not even the clerks of the board. We delayed the vote, left the boardroom, and went into private session.

Renne told us that the city couldn't afford the lawsuit. I'd introduced this legislation four months before, the testimony had concluded, and now—five minutes before the vote—the city attorney calls for a confidential meeting to tell us that we have to come up with a million dollars from the city budget before the resolution can pass.

I picture a mayor in the tobacco industry's pocket having a hasty and tense breakfast meeting with a compliant city attorney.

Under no condition was I going to allow this delaying tactic. I'd been fighting for this moment for years, and the public was outside waiting for us to vote on the lawsuit.

I've been in office long enough to know that an elected official has to have backing for a piece of legislation before it comes to a vote—especially legislation that can be derailed by money—and I had it. Eight of my colleagues' names were attached to this resolution as co-signers. There was no way they would suddenly change their minds under pressure from the city attorney. Sun-tzu stresses, in *The Art of War*, preparedness over all. I was prepared.

Three of my colleagues were outraged at this transparent attempt to quash the legislation. Board President Kevin Shelley called it sabotage, and the supervisors whose names were attached to the legislation refused to appear before the public and press and do a pro-tobacco about-face. Not in San Francisco. Not if the mayor was the Emperor of the World.

We walked back into the board chambers and passed the legislation without a single *no* vote.

Brown signed it.

However, we were still left with the lawsuit itself. I would have preferred that the city attorney do it. After all, the research had been done, and she had the staff. I certainly wouldn't have passed up the opportunity to prosecute a historical lawsuit if I were city attorney. But Brown and Renne decided to contract the lawsuit out to a private law firm that specializes in class-action lawsuits. They took the case on a contingency basis and the suit was filed a few days later.

With that filing, San Francisco became the first city in the country to sue the tobacco industry. Within two months, ten other counties, along with the cities of Los Angeles, Santa Barbara, San Diego, San Jose, New York City, and Chicago had all joined our lawsuit, as had the American Heart and Lung Society and three other organizations.

In September 1996, Willie Brown and Louise Renne were named Humanitarians of the Year by the local chapter of the American Cancer Society. They were honored for giving approval to San Francisco's lawsuit against the tobacco industry. This was the same Willie Brown who had taken more tobacco money than any other American politician in history. This was the same American Cancer Society that, in 1991, had made public a tobacco industry memo about Brown traveling to Louisville on industry money to discuss ways to get around local antismoking legislation. This was the same Willie Brown, jingling the pieces of silver in his pocket, who I believe had sent the city attorney to try to short-circuit the final board vote on the lawsuit.

The *San Francisco Examiner* summed up the award by saying, "That's like David Duke winning honors from the NAACP." Tobacco researcher Stanley Glantz called it "bizarre beyond words." Brown, however, was of another opinion, when he said, "I am a doer, not a talker. Awards go to doers, not talkers."

He was talking about me.

My last few months in office were dwindling down as a result of term limits, and I needed to get as much accomplished as I could. Earlier I had called for hearings to consider the licensing of cigarette retailers, increasing penalties for retailers who sell tobacco products to children, and banning all cigarette vending machines.

I had also introduced other legislation, such as an ordinance to prohibit the outdoor advertising and promotion of all tobacco products in publicly visible locations within a thousand feet of schools, parks, playgrounds, and recreation centers, even though the sheer number of such facilities would mean a virtual elimination of tobacco advertising in San Francisco. I have long believed that this is necessary, because the majority of advertising geared to children is being conducted at the local level. San Francisco has a huge number of corner markets, and there are Marlboro Men and Joe Camels hanging in the windows of nearly every one. These are the stores that children walk by on their way to and from school. These are the stores where children buy their candy and sodas. And what you see in almost every one is child-height window advertising, where Joe Camel lurks at the eye level of a typical prepubescent child.

The ads are a real problem in ethnic communities. A Latino boy from the Mission district testified at a city hearing, "It's aimed at us.

> It's not just the ads, it's where they're putting them. They're not all in the [affluent] Marina, with a store every three blocks. In the Mission there are stores on every corner. They're making money on our deaths.

I introduced this ordinance in 1995, but it went back to committee after the tobacco industry came in and showed us a map of San Francisco, pointing out that the geography of the restriction meant there would be no legal advertising left, and such a total ban was unconstitutional. Even limiting the ban to just schools and playgrounds would still have wiped out 90% of outdoor tobacco advertising in the city. That legislation, at this writing, is still in committee.

The Arab American Grocers Association also came to the hearings upset. This association has nearly 5,000 members, and each store gets anywhere from $3,000 to $20,000 each year from the tobacco industry—much of which is to keep these ads in their windows. The industry gladly pays this money, because the window ads are so effective at targeting children.

Of course, it's more complicated than just forcing signs out of the stores. The substantial money that small grocers receive from the tobacco industry is given in part for their agreeing to place displays on their counters. In October 1996 I authored an ordinance prohibiting self-service merchandising of tobacco products except in places to which minors have no access—another ordinance aimed at neighborhood markets. I'm not against grocers selling cigarettes, but one national study found that 22% of seventh-grade smokers stole cigarettes from counter displays. Even children without sticky fingers have counter displays right in their faces when they pay for their sodas.

It's a tough decision to ask a small, family-owned business to turn down the kind of money they were getting from the industry. In my committee and the final board hearings on this ordinance, I heard from several grocers. Each one who testified said he needed the money, that the $200 to $1,600 per month he got from the industry was vital to his survival. One said, "To deprive me of this small profit puts my business in jeopardy." Others described the importance of advertising, saying they would sell fewer cigarettes without the displays and signs. That may be, but the fact is that all cigarette sales should be done from behind the counter.

In the short run, obviously, getting children off cigarettes will hurt not just the industry, but merchants. There will be less tobacco money changing hands. But the bigger picture—one of decreasing health costs and consumer cash being spent on some other, less harmful indulgence, like candy—is what we need to focus on. My local grocer, Ibrahim Habash, has no self-service counter displays. He told me, "Angela, you're right. Children do steal cigarettes." In eliminating self-service, he said, "It's an inconvenience, but it's the right thing to do."

In November 1996, the board passed the ordinance prohibiting self-service merchandising and sent it on to Brown, who reluctantly signed it into law.

At the time our lawsuit was filed in San Francisco, nine states had filed their own suits against the tobacco industry. By October 1996, the number had risen to 15 states. Most of these have been for product liability, but others, like Texas, filed for fraud and RICO violations. In each case, jurisdictions are attempting to fight the industry by securing unreimbursed health-related expenditures.

The ultimate outcome of any of these suits is up in the air. The tobacco industry is proud of the fact that it has yet to pay a dime towards a judgment against it. They have the sharpest, most expensive attorneys on the planet. The enormous amount of money they shell out to fight the suits is nothing, however, compared to how much they'd have to pay if they lost even one state's class-action lawsuit.

This time around is a little different. The industry has given itself enough rope to hang by the neck: their own documents, research, perjury before Congress, and statements from former employees. The major tobacco companies, trade associations, and distributors have conspired for decades to mislead and deceive the public about the connection between smoking and disease and about the addictive nature of nicotine. Not only has the industry been engineering and selling a poisonous and addictive product, but it has been doing so by deceptive means, covering up their own research linking smoking with health problems. One company even used a research lab in Germany to perform work that the company was reluctant to perform in the U.S. There's also mounting evidence that the industry has for years used third parties to maintain sensitive documents for the purpose of preventing discovery in any lawsuit that is filed. They're hiding their own smoking guns. A lawsuit filed by Minnesota has shown that Philip Morris researchers destroyed and hid damning nicotine research conducted as early as the 1970s.

Evidence also suggests that cigarette companies have actually intended that their products contain a minimum level of nicotine to satisfy smokers' cravings—to keep 'em hooked. A senior Philip Morris scientist wrote in a confidential document made public in 1988, "Think of the cigarette as a dispenser for the dose unit of nicotine; smoke is the most optimized vehicle for dispensing nicotine." In the case of Brown & Williamson, however, engineering nicotine levels wasn't enough. Secret documents have shown that the company, while not necessarily increasing the amount of nicotine, adds ammonia compounds to tobacco in Marlboro cigarettes to intensify the potency of the nicotine present. Pending legislation that calls for an ingredient list on cigarette packaging would help to make the public aware of such content manipulation.

This evidence of an illegal cover-up is just the tip of the iceberg.

All of this evidence, crucial for the lawsuits to succeed, is what finally enabled the FDA to act in regard to tobacco. Dr. David Kessler, who served as the head of the FDA under Presidents Bush and Clinton, had been pushing to regulate cigarettes since 1990. His efforts, however, had to be put on hold until an irrefutable link between nicotine and addiction could be proved.

In summer 1994, Kessler got the evidence he needed when he was told by an advisory committee that nicotine was indeed an addictive drug and was the main reason people kept smoking. It was also postulated that if nicotine was removed from cigarettes, the number smoked in this country would drop from about 500 billion each year to about 25 billion, and at least ten million lives would be prolonged—at least one in four smokers dies prematurely.

Later in 1994, in Congressman Henry Waxman's House subcommittee hearings on tobacco, evidence was released that the industry was controlling the level of nicotine in cigarettes. The issue was no longer about the right of Americans to choose to use or ignore tobacco—Kessler stated that the industry was controlling the levels of nicotine in a way that "creates and sustains an addiction in the vast majority of smokers."

Starting to smoke is a matter of choice, but proof now exists that continuing to smoke is not. This reason alone is enough to come down with the entire weight of the federal government on the heads of tobacco industry executives.

This research enabled the Clinton administration and the FDA to declare war against the tobacco industry. In August 1996, the president announced that he supported the FDA's determination that cigarettes and smokeless tobacco are delivery devices for the drug nicotine. By identifying nicotine as an addictive drug, he gave the FDA authority to control the sale, distribution, and advertising of cigarettes and other tobacco products, and impose strict limits on the use of tobacco by minors.

President Clinton proposed several controls, all aimed at preventing children from smoking. Most of these are scheduled to go into effect in August 1997. As I did in my San Francisco legislation, the president proposed a ban on all cigarette vending machines in areas where minors have access, and a ban on all self-service displays. If the proposal holds, cigarettes will now be sold only by clerks over the counter and, as is the case with alcohol, customers will need to supply a photo ID for purchase.

Part of the Clinton proposal also requires the tobacco industry to fund a $150 million education campaign to prevent children from smoking, with a major emphasis on developing public service ads. Although the FDA has dropped the provision that the industry immediately set up this fund, it will likely have to cough up the money eventually.

The Clinton proposal also focuses on advertising. Like my hearings on outdoor advertising in publicly visible locations near schools, parks, playgrounds, and recreation facilities, Clinton's proposal similarly bans outdoor advertising and billboards, as well as any depictions, such as the Marlboro Man or Joe Camel, within one thousand feet of schools. Advertising restrictions also cover magazines read by teens. Any magazine ad is limited to black-and-white text only.

The proposal also forbids brand-name sponsorship of sporting events and advertising on such products as hats and T-shirts. The administration sees it the same way I do: to stop children from smoking, you have to remove images of cigarettes from the culture, from billboards, windows, magazines, clothing, and sporting events. The Association of National Advertisers claims that the regulations will not stand, but the free speech balance test, which allows some speech to be regulated—slander, for example, or obscene material—can be invoked in this case without lapsing into unconstitutionality, in my opinion.

Tobacco is ubiquitous. Whether it's the name *Marlboro* on the wall at Candlestick or Virginia Slims sponsoring a tennis tournament or a friendly, cigarette-proffering cartoon character painted on the floor of a corner market, a reminder that cigarettes are readily available is never far from our consciousness. Stanley Glantz has said, "The big battle now is getting tobacco industries out of politics and out of the arts."

Once the images of cigarettes are out of our line of sight, fewer people will smoke that first one. Fewer children. That's what really matters.

President Clinton has said about teen smoking,

This epidemic is no accident. Children are bombarded every day by massive advertising marketing campaigns that play to their vulnerabilities, their insecurities, their longing to be something in the world.

The fight against tobacco, though the toughest battle against industry that America has ever faced, will eventually prove successful. It shows that change is possible, and that dedicated individuals—from cancer researchers to determined politicians—can make a difference. The public's attitude is changing. If Willie Brown can see the writing on the wall and actually sign legislation to sue the industry, then there's hope that it can be accomplished elsewhere. There will be a cumulative effect.

We can't stop here. We have to step up the fight on as many fronts as possible. We can't get complacent. Remember, this industry is the most powerful one in America in terms of its lobbying influence; and there are still plenty of Willie Browns out there in positions of influence who are eager to take tobacco money. To keep winning, we must make such practices unacceptable. Americans must either vote tobacco-supporting politicians out of office or force them to change their views. We have to ensure that the FDA's regulations go into effect, and we have to look closely at any efforts to weaken them, such as the sweet-sounding, but ultimately tobacco-friendly, compromise suggested to Clinton by the industry in an attempt to keep the FDA off its back.

There's still more that can be done. Even if we don't make the tobacco industry accountable through lawsuits, we have to make sure that the advertising door is shut and will remain shut. This is critical, because if we can stop people from smoking, we can save lives, save health care costs, and eventually wipe out 90% of the domestic tobacco business.

This doesn't mean that tobacco companies will shut their doors. While overall domestic sales have decreased over recent years, the industry has continued to do what it is excellent at doing: finding other markets. If America is going to prevent the industry from targeting children, well, foreign markets are eager for American investment, even by tobacco companies. But we have to stay focused here; we can't do anything about industry "terrorism" abroad. Not yet. If we can succeed in the U.S., then perhaps we can provide a model for other nations, as we have in Great Britain.

In a career in which I have seen more than my share of heartbreaking defeats and thrilling victories, tobacco is my sweetest series of victories. The fight against the industry will succeed. People are more and more behind it. The drop in lung cancer rates in the last six years can be traced to the effectiveness of antitobacco campaigns. Even states in the tobacco belt have begun enacting antismoking ordinances. The higher question of the existence of the industry— the *morality* of its very continuation—is finally being discussed, and not simply on the fringe of politics.

Not smoking is the single most effective way a person can increase the length of his or her life. This issue belongs to the people, and our politicians must see that it stays in the limelight.

THE STARS

By that hidden way
My guide and I did enter, to return
To the fair world: and heedless of repose
We climb'd. . . .
We again beheld the stars.

INFERNO, CANTO XXXIV

WHEN I STARTED OUT IN POLITICS a decade ago, I wasn't thinking that I'd witness the Hell that resides beneath the surface. It's been a difficult journey and I've seen a lot of negatives—greed and corruption, thoughtless public officials, ravenous political machines, amoral corporations, and powerful and unethical lobbyists. These factors add up to a country with a morass of problems and a populace frustrated by the situation. This is a dangerous combination.

A frustrated voting public is also a mistrustful and apathetic one. Though our problems obviously did not all start in Vietnam or in the Nixon White House, we are left with the legacy of those assaults on our public trust. America is now so cynical about government and politicians that we even elect presidents that we don't find trustworthy. To be fair, though, our slate of presidential nominees has been terrible for at least a generation.

If America trusted Bob Dole slightly more than Bill Clinton, why didn't we elect him? Well, probably because we don't *expect* our politicians to be particularly trustworthy. Anyway, did anyone really believe that Bob Dole, cheerleader for Richard Nixon, powerful senator with ties to business—in a word, a *politician*—was more trustworthy than his opponent?

We say our leaders don't have to be particularly trustworthy as long as they get the job done. That's how Ronald Reagan or George Bush can become president—or Willie Brown can become mayor. We just want an *effective* leader, not necessarily an honest person.

We're paying a high price for that sentiment.

I probably haven't revealed or hinted at a single thing in these pages that will shock any reader who has ever thought about politics in a meaningful way. If a man helps his friend get elected mayor, who's surprised when the mayor steers lucrative city contracts his way? If an enormous private utility company is paying the re-election bills of half the politicians in the state, who's going to gasp in disbelief that the state legislature won't tighten utility regulations?

The stories and revelations of this book probably only confirm our already low expectations of government. But we *should* be gasping in disbelief. It's a sign of public apathy that these stories don't surprise us, let alone make us angry.

And public apathy is the force that allows the abuses and outrages to continue.

Politicians of both major parties have capitalized on our cynical view of government and are now calling for something called "less government." They propose tearing down the Department of Education, for example, or suspending regulation of our natural resources. Government, they say, should butt out of our private lives and out of business matters.

Unfortunately, less government usually means more abuses. That has been proven throughout history. At the turn of the century, America's food industry was rife with corruption and lax standards; people died. Government fixed the situation. In the 1950s, when segregation prohibited African Americans from participating in this country on any meaningful level, government intervened and struck down the Jim Crow laws. In the late 1960s and early 1970s, the automobile industry was operating out of control,, manufacturing dangerous cars and destroying the environment in the process. Government stepped in; America's auto industry is once again a world leader.

The list is endless. The only good government is not a dead one. Government, at its best, has made America the strongest and most prosperous nation on earth.

It's not fashionable in these conservative times to champion an activist government. But if you've accompanied me through the Hell

I've described in the last ten chapters, you know I rarely settle in comfortably with fashionable issues.

For everything wrong with local, state and national governments, we must remember what there is that works, what we should build on. There are committed people in government and the community who have the power and willingness to come together for the common good. I've seen honesty, caring, and dedication in the efforts of numerous community organizations across the country. I've witnessed it in the actions of volunteers who serve those with AIDS; who feed the homeless; who defend the needs of children, the mentally ill, and the sick; or who are part of the fight against crime, substance abuse, and tobacco. I've heard their voices in labor halls, on the phone, in committee hearings and at meetings of the board of supervisors. I've met them at police precincts, fire stations, children's centers, drug treatment facilities, and even in the corridors of city hall. Many have disagreed with me on specific issues but are still committed to fairness and justice; over the years both they and many others have said, "Give 'em hell, Angela."

Because of them I remain hopeful. But to effect a return to a government we trust, we must address the issues I've raised here—and many others.

I've described what happens when uncommitted politicians and bureaucrats are running the show. I've given examples of political pettiness, hand-washing, and arrogance. I've shown how vital services can be cut to spite other elected officials, and how lack of funding can keep police behind desks and prevent them from solving crimes. I've also discussed how the actions of indifferent bureaucrats often reflect a lack of concern and compassion for the feelings of victims of tragedy and their families, and how red tape and permit requirements can restrict citizens in the performance of their daily lives and prevent them from delivering services to needy populations like the mentally ill.

An uncommitted government hurts all of us. Uncommitted politicians strip us of our spirit and vitality, they reduce our desire to be involved in real issues, and they lower our expectations for improvement in the future. They prevent people from living their lives fully by adding to the rigidity of red tape and rules, by making minor problems difficult to solve, and by not going the extra mile to help those in need.

These are symptoms of a deeper underlying problem: the gulf between government and the people. The Hell I've described suggests that many public officials are already distant from the people and completely out of contact with their concerns, that the only commitment they have is to themselves or to those select groups that help maintain them in positions of power.

I don't know whether such public officials were uncommitted in the first place or if they became so only later, as a result of their involvement in government. If they were disconnected and distant when they began public life, then they certainly don't belong in office. Our leaders must focus at least as much on compassion as on performance. If one of the pitfalls of serving in office is detachment from the people, then we need to understand why this occurs and how to prevent it. In either case, there should be no room in public life for those who care little for the lives of the people. Caring should be the litmus test that voters apply to candidates.

Lack of commitment is a disease that spreads through the body politic. It's highly contagious and moves quickly from those in positions of power through the ranks of public service. What's worse, it can easily spread from government to the people. It's like Reagan's "trickle-down" theory—though in a form he would have denied. If we feel our politicians are cynical and cold, we begin to feel that way towards our politicians, then towards government in general. We vote with apathy or disdain, or worse: we don't vote at all.

This problem is not inherent in government or politics. Political institutions have the potential to work well, as they are starting to do in South Africa. The real source of the problem is a lack of visionary leaders. Unfortunately, politics can attract shortsighted and selfish people. While no one should be excluded from having a political voice, we must be aware of what politicians stand for: where is their money coming from? Who is pulling the strings? And we must demand that politicians focus on the business of governing.

The importance of visionary leadership cannot be overstated. It's difficult for any of us to maintain a vision of a better America in the future when there are few such visions being projected by our leaders. Without their visions our own visions become murky.

We certainly don't see this visionary spirit in people like Pete Wilson, Dan Lungren, or Newt Gingrich. Vision doesn't reside in the mean-spirited politics of division. We don't see it in the destruction of environmental protection or—in the name of "the family" —in attacks on poor women and children or in the decimation of the welfare system. Neither do we see vision in Dan Lungren's attack on those who support needle-exchange programs or in his raid on the San Francisco Cannabis Buyers' Club, the only source of help for many with life-threatening conditions.

Such mean-spirited politics may always be with us in one way or another, but occasionally, from somewhere, visionaries still find their way into public office.

The spirit of our American community thrives on the spirit of its public officials. This was the power of Kennedy, Roosevelt and Lincoln. We saw it when Mario Cuomo was governor of New York and when Pat Brown was governor of California. In San Francisco, we saw it in Harvey Milk in the gay community of the 1970s and in the actions of Dianne Feinstein, who brought the city together as the first woman mayor after the assassinations of Milk and Mayor George Moscone. That spirit was the legacy of Mayor "Sunny Jim" Rolph, who served from 1911 to 1930 and had the vision to provide for the future of San Francisco. He built the vast Hetch Hetchy water system and numerous other projects, from museums to water temples. It was also the legacy of my father, Joe Alioto, who inaugurated BART, altered San Francisco's skyline, and yet preserved the city's character and beauty.

When it makes itself known, this visionary spirit can spread like fire through government to the people. Committed officials can instill this vision in the rank and file of the government. They do it by their appointments and by keeping their doors open to employees and the public. They do it by instilling loyalty to the vision and to the public they serve, not by demanding loyalty to the powers that be. A committed official instills this loyalty not out of fear or mean-spiritedness, but out of the belief that government works best when ideas are rewarded, red tape and manipulative power are reduced, and the creative interplay between the public and government can move forward unimpaired.

Vision is the product of progressive, activist individuals in community and government. It necessarily involves moving forward. All of the greatest moments of American leadership were progressive and diametrically opposed to the standard "do-nothingism" of most politicians: the Emancipation Proclamation, the New Deal, the enforcement of integration in the South. These were progressive, visionary achievements.

This is also why machines fail us. Not only do they lower morale within government, but they freeze debate and interchange, quash creativity, and stamp out the spirit that exists among citizens. Though a few stated goals may be accomplished, major accomplishments are nearly impossible, because machine politicians' loyalty to power and money prevent them from working for the best interests of the people. Machines are, by their nature, regressive entities. The status quo is what allows them to flourish, and real progressive change diminishes their power.

It is with progressive politics that a vision of America's future lies. It cannot lie with fat-cat corporations running the country—we are close to that now, and a quarter of our children are living in poverty while racist, destructive companies rake in *trillions* of dollars a year. Neither can it lie with bombastic, backward-looking politicians who are proficient in turning the majority of their constituents against the minority rather than promoting the goal of living and working together as a community. Will the vision of our future be hate-filled: whites hating blacks, straight people hating gays and lesbians, everybody hating immigrants? True, Bob Dornan and several of his ultraconservative, ultra-hateful colleagues were voted out of office in 1996, but his ilk is still around.

We cannot settle for a vision of comfortable old men sitting in the offices of the Capitol. There are many congresspeople with the potential for a progressive vision, but when our leaders are left to their own devices, the vagaries of politics and elections preclude most of them making America better.

The vision must begin with us.

After Virgil led Dante past the source of all evil, Satan frozen in a lake at the bottom of Hell, the two climbed back up and out of the infernal regions, through a cave, and beheld the stars, which Dante had feared he would never see again.

In Dante's time, as in late-twentieth-century America, coming out of a dark place and seeing stars after you'd wondered whether you might never see them again—that's a powerful incentive to do what it takes to realize a vision of our future.

Stars are a good symbol for bringing about that vision. Our nation's founders envisioned America as a collection of stars—that's why they're on the flag. Kennedy moved us to look to the stars, not to our petty differences, for a vision of the future. And so we should.

In the long run, we are not a collection of differences—skin color, religion, sexual orientation, gender, ethnicity. We are all different, yes. America should and does celebrate those differences. But we are all neighbors, all Americans—all people.

239

I want us to finish this path through the dark woods that Dante defined so eloquently 700 years ago and that we are still traveling. Together we can describe a vision of the future, a progressive vision with a government that governs wisely and leaders that lead us *all* for the sake of America, and not for themselves.

We'll see the stars if we want to.

APPENDIX:
ALIOTO LEGISLATION, 1989-1997
(PARTIAL LISTING)

Resolution #336-91: Establish a Ballpark Advisory Committee to examine the building of a baseball park in downtown San Francisco in order to retain the Giants baseball franchise in San Francisco.

Resolution #727-92: Urging the Major League Baseball owners to keep the Giants baseball franchise in San Francisco.

Ordinance #165-93: Exempts poetry readings from entertainment permits required by City Police Code.

Ordinance #308-93: Prohibits the posting of signs on historic "path of gold" lampposts on Market Street.

Resolution #636-93: Creation of a Task Force on the African American Community to consider economic development issues for the African American Community in the Western Addition.

Resolution #1012-93: Creation of a Ballpark Committee for 7th and Townsend Streets to examine the possibility of building a baseball stadium in China Basin at 7th and Townsend Streets.

Resolution #887-93: Opposing Senate Bill 1185 regarding state preempting of landmark designations by municipalities in California.

Resolution #246-94: Renaming Price Row to Via Ferlinghetti in honor of Lawrence Ferlinghetti.

Ordinance #285-94: Amends the Planning Code to allow for the advertising on JCDecaux public toilets and public service kiosks.

Resolution #615-94: Opposing Assembly Bill 133 that prohibits municipalities from designating churches as landmarks.

Resolution #687-94: Approving the JCDecaux Public Toilet program.

Resolution #1089-95: Renaming one block of Green Street to Beach Blanket Babylon Boulevard in honor of Steve Silver.

Resolutions #208-96, 209-96 & 210-96: Opposing California ballot Propositions 200, 201 and 202 regarding tort liability, attorney's fees and tort cases.

Resolution #1026-96: Reaffirming the Sister City Relationship between San Francisco and Assisi, Italy.

ENVIRONMENTAL ISSUES

Resolution #929-89: Supporting the federal Ocean Protection Act (HR 3751).

Resolution #101-90: Supporting Assembly Bill 2603, regarding oil spill prevention.

Resolution #102-90: Supporting federal legislation regarding the San Francisco Bay Wetlands.

Resolution #799-90: Supporting federal legislation calling for an environmental review of the Presidio.

Resolution #214-91: Supporting Assembly Bill 854, the California Coastal Sanctuary Act of 1991.

Resolution #431-91: Supporting the federal Ancient Forest Protection Act of 1991 (HR 842).

Ordinance #164-92: Amends the Health Code regarding the placement and removal of underground storage tanks and hazardous materials.

Resolution #141-93: Urging adoption of state legislation regarding the San Francisco Bay Delta Estuary protections.

Resolution #886-93: Supporting the California Desert Protection Act (S. 21) and opposing any attempts to weaken the Act.

Resolution #450-94: Opposing the dredging of the waterfront area of the Marina district and the building of an additional breakwater.

Resolution #133-96: Opposing state legislation that would extend the usage of methyl bromide as a pesticide in California.

HEALTH AND HOMELESSNESS ISSUES

Resolution #164-90: Urging the United States government to remove travel restrictions on people with HIV/AIDS.

Resolution #174-90: Urging the state legislature to restore $15 million in cuts to community mental health services.

Resolution #296-90: Supporting the expenditure of state funds to test RU486 (the abortion pill) in the state of California.

Resolution #323-90: Supporting the federal Ryan White CARE Act of 1990

Resolution #129-91: Urging San Francisco to establish a policy opposing electroconvulsive therapy.

Resolution #131-91: Urging the United States government to remove HIV from INS exclusion for travel, immigration to the US.

Resolution #274-91: Supporting Assembly Bill 7, requiring that all motorcyclists wear safety helmets.

Resolution #305-91: Urging the state legislature to restore $100 million in substance abuse funding for the "Drug Waiting List Program."

Resolution #406-91: Urging the state legislature to allow testing and approval of new AIDS-related drugs through the California Food & Drug Branch Program.

Resolutions #80-92, 81-92, 82-92, 83-92, 84-92: Resolutions establishing San Francisco's needle exchange program.

Resolution #482-92: Urging the state legislature to increase the number of AIDS-related drugs made available through the AIDS Drug Assistance Program.

Resolution #867-92: Condemning Governor Wilson's veto of state legislation supporting and allowing needle exchange programs.

Ordinance #98-93: Establishing the San Francisco Mental Health Board.

Resolution #155-93: Opposing federal legislation reversing recent regulations lifting travel restrictions barring people with HIV/AIDS from entering the United States.

Resolution #160-93: Urging the federal government to allow Haitian refugees living with HIV entry into the US for medical care.

Resolution #278-93: Supporting Assembly Bill 260, allowing needle exchange programs in San Francisco.

Resolution #512-93: Opposing Senate Bill 1239 regarding mandatory AIDS testing.

Resolution #637-93: Urging state legislature to allow the medical use of marijuana.

Resolution #835-93: Condemning Governor Wilson's veto of state legislation regarding needle exchange programs.

Resolution #923-93: Urging the US Congress to reclassify marijuana from a Schedule I drug and allow physicians to prescribe medicinal marijuana.

Resolution #924-93: Urging the San Francisco Department of Public Health to add medicinal marijuana into its master plan for substance abuse and HIV treatment.

Resolution #43-94: Urging the Federal Department of Health & Human Services to provide public service commercials regarding condom use and HIV targeted to gay and bisexual males.

Resolution #179-94: Opposing Senate Bill 1432 that would classify HIV/AIDS as a venereal disease.

Resolution #204-94: Urging the federal government to designate San Francisco's public health clinics as federally qualified primary care clinics.

Resolution #298-94: Urging the Department of Public Health's AIDS Office to allow public input and consultation regarding the release of epidemiological studies regarding AIDS cases in San Francisco.

Resolution #376-94: Creating the HIV Youth Advisory Task Force to provide policy and program recommendations to the board of supervisors and mayor.

Resolution #442-94: Urging the San Francisco Department of Public Health to conduct tests for lead poisoning at the Geneva Towers public housing unit.

Resolution #729-94: Urging the United States Congress to pass legislation lifting the ban on public funding of needle exchange programs.

Resolution #730-94: Urging the United States Congress to pass legislation allowing for the medicinal use of marijuana.

Resolution #1003-94: Restoring full funding for the Department of Public Health's Center for Special Problems (CSP), ensuring continuation of the CSP's unique mental health services.

Resolution #137-95: Urging the U. S. Congress to reauthorize the Ryan White CARE Act and to increase funding for AIDS treatment, care and housing.

Resolution #186-95: Supporting Assembly Bill 1529 that allows for the possession and medical use of marijuana.

Resolution #263-95: Opposing state legislation calling for the mandatory name reporting of people with HIV/AIDS.

Resolution #309-95: Supporting Assembly Bill 1408 that would allow for the compassionate release of prisoners in the final stages of a terminal illness (AIDS, cancer).

Resolution #310-95: Opposing Senate Bill 889 that would require mandatory HIV testing of newborn infants.

Resolution #311-95: Opposing federal legislation that would require mandatory HIV testing of newborn infants.

Resolution #426-95: Urging the appointment of mental health & substance abuse "czar" for the San Francisco Department of Public Health.

Resolution #469-95: Urging the expansion of City employee health plans to include coverage of Traditional Chinese Medicine and alternative therapies.

Resolution #485-95: Opposing the closure of the Department of Public Health's Tom Smith Center that provides substance abuse and alcohol treatment services.

Resolution #1041-95: Urging the major television networks to carry public service announcements regarding condom use & HIV transmission.

Resolution #1079-95: Supporting federal legislation (HR 2816) that would allow marijuana to be used for medicinal purposes.

Resolution #114-96: Urging the governor and state legislature to increase funding for the state "AIDS Drug Assistance Program" and to approve the addition of newly approved drugs to the ADAP list.

Resolution #134-96: Opposing federal legislation that requires mandatory discharge of all HIV-positive military personnel.

Resolution# 312-96: Opposing Assembly Bill 2147 that would require anyone with HIV to disclose their status to any sexual partner; failure to provide this information would be a felony.

Resolution #314-96: Supporting Senate Bill 1976 that would allow needle exchange programs.

Resolution #407-96: Urging the Department of Public Health to provide sexual assault services specific to the needs of young girls.

Resolution #578-96: Urging Mayor Willie Brown to direct all city agencies to refrain from building power generation plants in Bayview-Hunters Point .

Resolution #733-96: Opposing federal legislation (HR 3937) regarding HIV testing mandates.

HOUSING AND WELFARE ISSUES

Resolution #322-91: Opposing Governor Wilson's cuts to AFDC benefits and urging the state legislature to increase funding for AFDC by at least 9%.

Resolution #1083-91: Opposing proposed reductions in AFDC benefits.

Resolution #42-94: Opposing Governor Wilson's proposed cuts to AFDC benefits.

Resolution #274-94: Opposing Assembly Bill 1320 regarding state preemption of local rent control laws.

Ordinance #1-95: Exempts loans as income when applying for General Assistance.

Resolution #214-95: Opposing Mayor Jordan's "Matrix Program" and urging the Mayor to immediately end the Matrix Program as a solution to dealing with homelessness.

Resolution #236-95: Opposing Assembly Bill 1257 regarding state preemption of local rent control laws.

LABOR AND BUSINESS ISSUES

Ordinance #425-89: Creating the San Francisco Film and Video Arts Commission.

Resolution #174-91: Establishing a task force to examine the issue of interim zoning controls regarding large-scale drugstore chains in city neighborhoods.

Ordinance #272-93: Amends the planning code section regarding coffee houses.

Resolution #361-93: Creation of a Task Force on Local Employment Opportunities.

Resolution #217-94: Creation of a Local Contracting and Hiring Task Force to examine the issue of contracts being awarded to out-of-state companies at the expense of local businesses.

Resolution #156-95: Opposing the closure and demolition of the North Beach Parking Garage due to the impact on businesses and residents of North Beach and Chinatown.

File #176-96-009 (no Resolution # at this date): Urging the San Francisco Symphony management to reinstate health benefits for striking members of the San Francisco Musicians Union.

LESBIAN AND GAY RIGHTS ISSUES

Resolution #7-91: Supporting state legislation calling for lesbian, gay & bisexual sensitivity training of police officers.

Resolution #968-92: Supporting the 1993 March on Washington for Lesbian/Gay/Bisexual & Transgender Rights.

Resolution #46-93: Resolution urging the federal government to end its policy of discrimination based on sexual orientation in the military.

Resolution #171-94: Urging the Civil Service Commission to adopt rules that provide family leave and medical care benefits to domestic partners.

Resolution #174-94: Condemning the Reverend Fred Phelps for his vicious attacks on the lesbian and gay community and people with HIV/AIDS.

Resolution #271-94: Supporting Assembly Bill 2810 that would establish state recognition of domestic partnerships.

Resolution #285-94: Supporting the Stonewall 25th International March for Lesbian/Gay Rights.

Resolution #816-94: Condemning Governor Wilson's veto of Assembly Bill 2810 that would have established state recognition of domestic partnerships.

Resolution #82-96: Opposing Assembly Bill 1982 that would prohibit recognition of same-sex marriages by the state of California.

Resolution #313-96: Opposing Assembly Bill 3227 that would prohibit recognition of same-sex marriages by the state of California.

Resolution #316-96: Supports federal legislation reauthorizing the Hate Crime Statistics Act (S. 1624).

Resolution #447-96: Opposing the federal "Defense of Marriage Act" (HR 3396) that allows the federal government and state governments the option of not recognizing legal same-sex marriages.

PUBLIC POWER ISSUES

Resolution #389-94: Supporting the use and sale of local, public electrical power and urging the Mayor and the PUC to aggressively bid for the National Park Service contract for the generation of electricity at the Presidio.

Resolution #863-94: Authorizing San Francisco to join Women's Energy, Inc. in its protest of the National Park Service's Presidio power bid award.

Resolution #963-94: Urging the Mayor and the PUC to explore a franchise fee increase for PG&E's use of city streets to provide electrical power & gas to its customers.

Ordinance #90-95: Amending the Administrative Code to require the PUC to prepare and transmit to the Board of Supervisors a preliminary report regarding the feasibility of municipalizing the electricity utilities distribution system in San Francisco.

Resolution #251-95: Urging the mayor and the PUC to request that the City Attorney immediately file an appeal to overturn the National Park Service's award to PG&E to provide electrical power to the Presidio.

Resolution #1091-95: Urging the mayor and the PUC to terminate immediately the contract with Strategic Energy Ltd. for the municipalization study and to review and reevaluate the contractor selection process.

Resolution #604-96: Urging the PUC to terminate its contract with ETAG to prepare a preliminary feasibility study regarding the municipalization of the electricity utilities system in San Francisco.

PUBLIC SAFETY ISSUES

Resolution #102-92: Supporting Assembly Bills 2264 and 2265 regarding sexual harassment.

Ordinance #364-93: Amends Police Code to require notification of potential victims upon release of convicted stalkers in San Francisco.

Resolution #384-93: Supporting federal legislation establishing a "Life-three-strikes" penalty for convicted felons.

Resolution #728-93: Urging the state legislature to increase penalties and change the definition of stalking; and to provide notice to victims of stalking upon release of stalker.

Resolution #39-94: Urging state legislature to increase penalties for child abduction.

Ordinance #90-94: Amends Police Code by creating "Aggressive Pursuit" of individuals as a crime.

Resolution #135-94: Urging the state legislature to increase penalties for aggressive pursuit and stalking.

Resolution #195-94: Urging state legislature to increase penalties for trespassing on the Golden Gate Bridge.

Resolution #226-94: Supporting Assembly Bill 37X, prohibiting the sale and/or possession of semi-automatic weapons in the state of California.

Resolution #349-94: Urging a reward of $10,000 be posted for information regarding the murder of Justin Jones.

Resolution #440-94: Urging a reward of $10,000 be posted for information regarding the murder of Alexis McNeal.

Resolution #1021-94: Urging the Police Commission and the Police Dept. to provide semi-automatic weapons for San Francisco police officers.

Resolution #1030-94: Supporting state legislation regarding increased penalties for carrying loaded firearms.

Resolution #129-95: Urging an increase in the reward offered for information regarding the murder of Tony Ray, from $10,000 to $25,000.

Resolution #404-96: Urging the state legislature to increase the penalties for the crime of rape and to increase funding for rape prevention & counseling services.

Resolution #1047-96: Creation of a Sexual Assault Task Force to examine and recommend improvement of sexual assault services for young girls.

TOBACCO ISSUES

Ordinance #234-91: Prohibits the placement of cigarette vending machines in San Francisco except in places to which minors have no access.

Ordinance #186-92: Prohibits the advertisement of tobacco products on property owned by the City and County of San Francisco.

Resolution #655-91: Supporting Senate Bill 376 relating to tobacco control in the state of California.

Resolution #476-92: Urging all city boards, commissions and departments to request individuals and entities currently enjoying advertising rights on city property to stop advertising cigarettes and tobacco products and to renegotiate leases, permits and agreements to ban advertising of tobacco and cigarette products.

Ordinance #359-93: Prohibits smoking in all workplaces, restaurants and sports arenas in the City and County of San Francisco. (This legislation was amended to change certain language by Ordinance #249-94)

Resolution #413-93: Regarding state legislation related to local smoking restrictions.

Resolution #293-94: Supporting proposed changes in the federal OSHA regulations to ban smoking in the workplace.

Resolution #437-94: Urging the removal of all cigarette advertising from Candlestick Park.

Resolution #819-94: Opposing California Proposition 188, the California Uniform Tobacco Control Act that would eliminate local tobacco control ordinances.

Resolution #920-94: Supporting the national petition drive to have tobacco products regulated by the federal Food and Drug Administration.

Resolution #931-95: Supporting President Clinton's and the FDA's plan to reduce smoking among youth through regulation of tobacco products.

Resolution #58-96: Supporting Assembly Bill XX55 that would allow local jurisdictions to establish a local cigarette excise tax.

Resolution #1030-95: Urging the Police Department to increase enforcement of laws prohibiting the sale of tobacco products to minors.

Resolution #386-96: Urging the San Francisco Retirement Board to divest holdings in securities of publicly traded companies that derive revenue from the sale of tobacco products and urging the state legislature to pass legislation barring state and municipal pension funds from holding tobacco stocks.

Ordinance #446-96: Amends the Police Code to prohibit self-service merchandising of tobacco products except in places to which minors have no access.

Resolution #458-96: Urging the state legislature to amend California Civil Code section 1714.45 that immunizes tobacco manufacturers from consumer product liability lawsuits filed in California.

Resolution #469-96: Urging the City Attorney and District Attorney to institute litigation against the US tobacco companies to recover costs of caring for people with smoking-related illnesses.

Resolution #499-96: Supporting federal legislation (HR 969) that would prohibit smoking on any scheduled airline flight segment in intrastate, interstate or foreign air travel.

Resolution #500-96: Urging the Food and Drug Administration to establish regulations requiring the listing of all ingredients contained in cigarettes on all cigarette packaging.

Resolution #501-96: Urging the Food and Drug Administration to establish regulations requiring the rating of tar & nicotine levels contained in cigarettes.

Resolution #612-96: Urging the California state attorney general to institute litigation against the US tobacco companies to recover the costs of caring for people with smoking-related illnesses.

Resolution #629-96: Opposing proposed restrictions in the state FY 1996-97 budget or any implementing legislation that restricts Prop. 99 tobacco research and media programs.

Resolution #732-96: Supporting state Constitutional Resolution 62 urging the California state Attorney General to file a civil action against tobacco companies to recover the costs of caring for people with smoking-related illnesses.

Resolution #819-96: Supporting the Food and Drug Administration's rules regulating tobacco products and advertising.

Resolution #985-96: Urging the state legislature to amend state law to allow the creation of local licensing schemes for retail tobacco sales.

Resolution #986-96: Urging the state legislature to increase penalties for selling tobacco products to minors.

Ordinance # -96 (not yet assigned): Prohibiting cigarette vending machines in San Francisco, even in places where minors are not permitted by law.

TAINTED MILLION

ISBN 0-9653524-1-2 $11.95

BY SUSAN TROTT

Jenny Hunt only wants the simple things in life—a house in a small town, one or two close friends, and to paint. But when her former lover takes a dive off the Golden Gate Bridge and leaves her an ill-gotten million dollars, offbeat characters start coming out of the woodwork.

"Hilarious . . . a delightful little read."   —*San Francisco Examiner*

SWAMP CATS

ISBN 0-9653524-0-4 $11.95

BY JEFF LOVE

R.E.M.? Forget them. Hootie and the Blowfish? Pop lightweights. Make room in your CD rack for Swamp Cats—the most unlikely rock group to almost explode onto the *Billboard* charts.

"Love is a writer with a future."   —*San Francisco Review*

FUNERALS FOR HORSES

ISBN 0-9653524-3-9 $19.95

BY CATHERINE RYAN HYDE

The gritty, compelling tale of a woman's search for her lost childhood. When her brother disappears, leaving behind his family, his money, and even the clothes he was wearing, Ella Ginsberg abandons a dying group of friends and lovers and undertakes a personal mission to bring him back and, with him, her tenuous grip on reality.

To order, indicate title and send the cover price plus $2.00 shipping and handling to:

RUSSIAN HILL PRESS
6410 GEARY BOULEVARD
SAN FRANCISCO, CA 94121